HOW TO HEAL FROM NARCISSISTIC ABUSE

LEARN TO RECOGNIZE MANIPULATION TACTICS, RECOVER FROM EMOTIONAL TRAUMA, AND RECLAIM YOUR INDEPENDENCE

JACKSON PORTER

CONTENTS

INTRODUCTION

Picture this: It's a chilly afternoon, and you're sitting across from your partner at your favorite café. The air is filled with the aroma of freshly brewed coffee, and the gentle hum of conversation provides a comforting backdrop to your intimate tête-à-tête. As you sip your latte, you feel a sense of contentment wash over you. Everything seems normal until your partner's words cut through the tranquility like a sharp knife.

"You're too sensitive," they say, their tone dismissive and their words like a slap in the face. You freeze, the warmth of the café fading into the background as their words echo in your mind. In an instant, the world you thought you knew crumbles around you, leaving you feeling exposed and vulnerable.

Perhaps you're still in the throes of this toxic relationship, trapped in a cycle of manipulation and emotional abuse. Every interaction with your partner leaves you walking on eggshells, afraid to speak your mind or express your true feelings for fear of their wrath. You constantly question your perceptions, wondering if you're as sensitive as they claim or if something is inherently wrong with you.

Or maybe you've already mustered the courage to leave, to break free from the suffocating grip of narcissistic abuse. You've taken the first steps toward reclaiming your autonomy and rebuilding your life, but the scars of your past still linger, haunting your every step. The memories of their gaslighting, their manipulation, their relentless invalidation of your feelings—they refuse to fade away, a constant reminder of the pain you endured.

Remember our journey together through *How to Stop Being Toxic*? We explored the depths of toxic behavior, understanding its roots and empowering ourselves to break free from harmful patterns. Now, let's take that knowledge and dive even deeper into a specific type of toxicity that can wreak havoc on our lives: narcissistic abuse.

Now, in *How to Heal from Narcissistic Abuse*, we're taking our exploration a step further by focusing specifically on the insidious effects of narcissistic behavior within relationships. While toxic behavior encompasses a range of harmful actions, narcissistic abuse operates on a deeper level by exploiting vulnerabilities and systematically dismantling the victim's sense of self.

I see you sitting there with a weight on your shoulders that feels impossible to shake off. Maybe you're grappling with the emotional turmoil of a toxic relationship, where every interaction leaves you questioning your worth and sanity. Or perhaps you're haunted by the memories of gaslighting and manipulation, second-guessing your every thought and feeling. Whatever your situation, I want you to know that I understand.

I understand the isolation and loneliness that come with narcissistic abuse as the manipulator chips away at your connections with friends, family, and even yourself. I understand the constant self-doubt and second-guessing as you struggle to trust your instincts and judgments in the face of relentless invalidation. I understand the deep sense of despair and hopelessness that can accompany the aftermath of narcissistic abuse as you grapple with the haunting symptoms of PTSD that linger long after the relationship ends.

You are not alone in your pain. Many have been there, too, trapped in the suffocating grip of narcissistic abuse, wondering if there was a way out. And I'm here to tell you that there is. Together, we'll navigate the complexities of narcissistic behavior, uncovering the tactics used to control and manipulate and offering practical tools for breaking free from the cycle of abuse.

Allow me to introduce myself: I'm Jackson Porter, the voice behind the words you'll find on these pages. As someone who has personally experienced the devastating effects of narcissistic abuse, I bring a unique perspective and firsthand understanding to the table.

I've walked the rocky road of toxic relationships, grappling with the emotional turmoil, self-doubt, and isolation that accompany narcissistic abuse. But through my journey of healing and self-discovery, I've emerged stronger and more resilient than ever before. This journey, coupled with my personal development background, lends credibility to my words.

So, why did I choose to write this book? It's simple: I believe no one should have to suffer in silence. I've seen firsthand the damage that narcissistic abuse can inflict, and I'm passionate about offering a lifeline to those who are still struggling. My goal is to provide you with the guidance, support, and tools you need to break free from the cycle of abuse and reclaim your sense of self-worth.

But beyond that, I wrote this book because I believe in the power of transformation. I've seen firsthand the incredible resilience of the human spirit, and I know healing is possible, even in the face of seemingly insurmountable odds.

In this book, I present a comprehensive solution to navigating narcissistic abuse in five crucial steps. These steps serve as a roadmap for understanding, leaving, healing, moving on, and preventing future toxic relationships.

This book delivers the solution of navigating narcissistic abuse through the comprehensive *BREAKOUT* framework. By following this framework, you will:

- Understand abuse dynamics
- Heal emotional wounds and rebuild self-esteem
- Regain a strong sense of self and identity
- Trust your instincts and judgments confidently
- Establish healthy boundaries in all relationships
- Experience a newfound sense of peace and inner calm
- Cultivate fulfilling connections with supportive individuals
- Fully recover from the traumatic experience you've had in your toxic relationships

- Successfully move on without relapsing or going back to your old toxic partners, friends, work relationships, and more

This is how our framework works:

B: Break the façade. Uncover the mask of manipulation and control worn by the narcissist, freeing yourself from their deceitful facade.

R: Release yourself from the chains of manipulation and codependency. Break the chains that bind you to the narcissist, reclaiming your independence and autonomy.

E: Escape the narcissist's traps safely. Navigate your way out of the narcissist's traps, protecting yourself from further harm.

A: Acknowledge the aftermath. Face the consequences of narcissistic abuse head-on, accepting the pain and trauma while paving the way for healing.

K: Keep yourself holistically healthy. Prioritize your well-being and nurture your mind and spirit as you embark on the recovery journey.

O: Own your narrative. Take back control of your story, reclaiming your sense of self and identity after abuse.

U: Unravel and fix negative patterns. Unriddle the adverse patterns and beliefs instilled by the narcissist, replacing them with healthier, more empowering ones.

T: Transcend past wounds and build healthy relationships. Build healthy, fulfilling relationships built on trust, respect, and mutual support.

After reading this book and implementing its framework, you'll step into a life transformed—a life filled with newfound confidence, inner peace, and fulfilling connections.

In your relationships, you'll experience a profound shift. No longer will you tolerate toxic dynamics or settle for less than you deserve. Instead, you'll set firm boundaries and surround yourself with supportive individuals who lift you up and celebrate your authenticity. You'll build deep, meaningful connections built on trust, respect, and mutual understanding.

Gone are the days of second-guessing yourself and doubting your instincts. You'll trust yourself implicitly, confident in your ability to discern healthy from unhealthy, genuine from manipulative. Your self-esteem will soar as you recognize your inherent value and embrace your true worth.

Before discovering the insights in this book, achieving this level of liberation and empowerment may have felt like an insurmountable challenge. The information presented here offers hope in what may have felt like a sea of darkness. It provides a roadmap—a guiding light—that illuminates the path to healing and growth.

Without this invaluable knowledge, you may have remained trapped in the cycle of narcissistic abuse, unable to break free from its suffocating grasp. But armed with the tools and understanding provided in these pages, you're empowered to reclaim your life, rewrite your story, and create a future filled with joy, fulfillment, and boundless possibilities.

So, if you're ready to embrace transformation, reclaim your sense of self-worth, and live a life free from the shadows of abuse, trust me when I say this is the right book for you. You're not alone, and brighter days are just around the corner.

CHAPTER 1
B—BREAK THE FACADE

"Over and over again, I have learned how damaging and unrelenting the aftermath of these pathological, quietly undermining relationships is."

SANDRA BROWN

As Hilda sat alone in her car, her hands gripping the steering wheel with white-knuckled intensity, she struggled to hold back the tears that threatened to spill over. She had just left another heated argument with her partner, Logan, and the echoes of his harsh words still rang in her ears like a relentless drumbeat.

Their relationship had once been a whirlwind romance filled with passion and promise. But as time wore on, Hilda began to notice a subtle shift in Logan's behavior—a gradual erosion of the love and respect that had once defined their connection.

The tipping point came one evening when Logan exploded in a fit of rage, hurling insults and accusations at Hilda with a ferocity that left her reeling. "You're so pathetic," he sneered, his voice dripping with contempt. "No one else would ever put up with you."

Hilda felt her heart shatter into a million pieces as she listened to Logan's cruel tirade, his words crushing her spirit. She had always believed that love was supposed to lift you up, not tear you down, but now she found herself trapped in a toxic cycle of manipulation and abuse.

As she drove aimlessly through the darkened streets, Hilda knew that she couldn't continue down this destructive path any longer. She deserved better than this—she deserved a life filled with kindness, compassion, and unconditional love.

WHAT IS NARCISSISTIC ABUSE?

People tend to throw the word "narcissism" around in casual conversation, often in contexts where it may not fully apply. However, it's imperative to truly understand what narcissistic abuse is and how it differs from simply exhibiting self-centered behavior. Narcissistic abuse goes beyond self-absorption—it's a pattern of manipulation, control, and exploitation that can have devastating effects on its victims.

Imagine a situation where Stephanie is in a relationship with Kyle. At first, Kyle's charm and charisma drew Stephanie in, and she felt like she had found her perfect partner. But as time went on, Kyle's behavior began to change. He became increasingly critical of Stephanie, belittling her achievements and dismissing her opinions. Whenever Stephanie tried to express her feelings or needs, Kyle would gaslight her, making her doubt her sanity and perceptions.

As the relationship progressed, Kyle's manipulation escalated. He would use guilt trips and emotional blackmail to get his way, leaving Stephanie feeling like she was walking on eggshells around him. He isolated her from her friends and family, convincing her that he was the only one who truly understood and cared for her.

In this relationship, Kyle's behavior exemplifies narcissistic abuse. He uses tactics such as gaslighting, manipulation, and isolation to maintain control over Stephanie and fulfill his selfish desires. This type of abuse is insidious, as it slowly erodes your sense of self-worth and autonomy, leaving you feeling trapped and powerless.

Narcissistic abuse presents itself in several forms beyond gaslighting, manipulation, and isolation. There are various ways in which narcissistic abuse manifests in our relationships, whether they be friendships, romantic partnerships, or family dynamics. Understanding these different forms of narcissistic abuse is crucial for recognizing and addressing toxic behaviors in our interpersonal connections.

One common form of narcissistic abuse is emotional blackmail. Jack and Emma have been friends for years. Jack often uses emotional blackmail to manipulate Emma into doing things for him. For example, when Emma tries to set boundaries or prioritize her needs, Jack often responds by guilt-tripping her and making her feel bad about her decisions. Emma feels trapped and unable to assert herself, fearing losing Jack's approval and support.

Another insidious form of narcissistic abuse is invalidation. This is common within our family bonds. I believe some of us, in the past, have confided in our parents about our struggles at work or within our romantic relationships. We shared with the optimism that our parents would offer empathy and a couple of kind words, but instead, they always disregarded our feelings and simply said, "Just get over it," or, "Stop being so sensitive." This is what invalidation looks like and usually leads us to doubt the validity of our emotions and experiences.

Narcissistic abuse can also take the form of manipulation through flattery and love bombing. In our previous book, we discussed what love bombing looks like, and we can agree that many of us are guilty when it comes to this. When we have just met someone new and develop feelings toward them, we tend to behave in a charming manner to win them over through gifts, lovely gestures, and all sorts of sweet things. However, as the relationship progresses, our behavior can become increasingly controlling and demanding as we grow to utilize flattery and love bombing as tools to manipulate others into complying with our wishes, leaving them feeling confused and emotionally drained.

In many common scenarios, narcissistic abuse can manifest as financial exploitation. A friend of mine, Rachel, shared an ordeal about how her older brother, David, constantly asks her for money, promising to pay her back but never following through. David is quite aware of Rachel's sense of familial obligation, and he leverages her kindness to extract financial support from her, leaving her feeling taken advantage of and financially drained.

While researching the most common forms of narcissistic abuse in relationships, I learned that withholding is quite a big issue. This is where the abuser intentionally withholds affection, attention, or resources as a means of exerting control. Some people feel that withholding can be a form of communication to pass an unsaid message across to their partner, but in a true sense, they are just being abusive. For instance, some men mention that when they are tired of their partner and are afraid of breaking up with them formally, they resort to withholding tactics with the incentive that their partner will read the room and move away. This creates feelings of anxiety and insecurity about the relationship, leaving their partners constantly on edge, desperate for validation and approval.

In some cases, narcissistic abuse escalates to physical violence or aggression, and this is quite often the hallmark of narcissistic abuse. For instance, some partners resort to physical violence when they feel threatened or challenged. They use their size and strength to intimidate their partners, leaving them feeling powerless and terrified for their safety. The constant fear of violent outbursts keeps them trapped in the abusive relationship, unable to leave for fear of further harm. However, physical violence is not limited to the bigger or stronger partner, as it is becoming more common that the partners less expected to be violent are actually the violent ones.

As we can see from these scenarios, narcissistic abuse takes on several forms, and our experiences may vary. Sometimes, we may not even recognize we are being subjected to narcissistic abuse because the narcissists are adept at portraying themselves as good people. However, one thing stands out: Narcissistic abuse is quite common, and it's essential to understand how to identify the subtle signs of this behavior.

This leads us to explore the signs that you may be a victim of narcissistic abuse. When you recognize these signs, you can begin to untangle yourself from the web of manipulation and reclaim your sense of self-worth and autonomy.

Signs You're a Victim

One of the signs that you may be a victim of narcissistic abuse is if you find yourself experiencing dissociation as a survival mechanism. Now, what does that mean exactly? It means that when things get tough, you sort of mentally check out to cope with the overwhelming stress and emotional turmoil.

Picture this: You're in yet another heated argument with your partner, and the tension is so thick you could cut it with a knife. Suddenly, it's like you're not even there anymore—you're just going through the motions, numb to the chaos around you. You might even feel like you're watching the scene play out from a distance, disconnected from your emotions and thoughts.

Dissociation might seem like a handy escape route in the moment, but in reality, it's just another way that the narcissist's toxic behavior is taking its toll on you. It's a sign that you're struggling to cope with the constant stress and emotional manipulation, and it's not something to brush off lightly.

Some of us walk on eggshells in our relationships, right? Now, I'm not talking about tiptoeing around a delicate situation occasionally—I'm talking about feeling like you're constantly walking on a minefield, never knowing when the next explosion will happen.

When you're at home with your partner, you often find yourself being a little more careful and choosing your words and actions with the precision of a tightrope walker. You're hyper-aware of their moods and triggers and go out of your way to avoid setting them off. Maybe you even find yourself apologizing profusely for things that aren't your fault just to keep the peace.

Walking on eggshells like this is exhausting, both mentally and emotionally. It's like living in a constant state of fear and anxiety, never knowing when the next outburst is going to happen. And let me tell you, nobody deserves to live like that.

Do you ever find yourself putting your basic needs and desires on the back burner, sacrificing your emotional and even physical safety just to please the abuser? It's a tough question but an important one to ask yourself. We all want to make our loved ones happy, but there's a big difference between compromising and neglecting your well-being.

You may find yourself in a relationship with someone who always wants things done their way. They belittle your wants and needs, making you feel like you don't matter. So, you constantly bend over backward to accommodate your partner, even if it means sacrificing your happiness and safety in the process.

Maybe you skip meals because they're too busy to eat with you, or you suppress your emotions because they can't handle anything that doesn't revolve around them. Perhaps you even put yourself in dangerous situations because they guilt-trip you into doing things you know aren't right. If you find yourself constantly putting your own needs on the back burner to keep peace with the narcissist in your life, it's time to take a step back and reevaluate your priorities.

Our bodies have a way of expressing what our minds may not always be able to articulate, and when you're in an emotionally toxic environment, it takes a toll on your physical health. You may start feeling constantly fatigued or experience headaches, stomachaches, or other unexplained physical symptoms. No matter how many doctor's appointments you schedule or medications you try, nothing seems to alleviate the discomfort. It's like your body is screaming for help, but you can't figure out what's wrong.

These physical symptoms may be a manifestation of the psychological turmoil you're experiencing due to the narcissistic abuse. Your body is essentially sounding the alarm, trying to alert you that something isn't right in your environment. It's a way of coping with the stress and trauma that you may not even realize you're enduring.

If you find yourself struggling with unexplained health issues or somatic symptoms, it's essential to consider the role that your environment and relationships may be playing. Your body is trying to tell you something, and it's crucial to listen to what it's saying.

Another telltale sign that you may be a victim of narcissistic abuse is if you develop a pervasive sense of mistrust. When you're constantly subjected to manipulation, gaslighting, and deceit, you naturally become wary and suspicious of others' intentions.

Picture this: You're in a relationship where your partner constantly lies to you, twists the truth, and undermines your sense of reality. Over time, you question everything and everyone around you. You find yourself second-guessing people's motives, wondering if they have ulterior motives or hidden agendas. Even the people closest to you, whom you once trusted implicitly, now seem suspect.

This pervasive sense of mistrust can seep into every aspect of your life, making it difficult to form genuine connections and maintain healthy relationships. You may find yourself withdrawing from social interactions, keeping people at arm's length to protect yourself from potential harm.

Some of us may struggle to understand the lengths to which narcissistic abuse can take us, and believe me, it can get as bad as suicidal ideation. When you're trapped in a toxic relationship where your needs are constantly disregarded and your worth is undermined, it can take a devastating toll on your mental health.

When you're in a relationship where your partner constantly tears you down, belittles your accomplishments, and makes you feel like you're worthless, the constant barrage of criticism and manipulation leaves you feeling utterly hopeless and overwhelmed. You could start to entertain thoughts of ending your own life, believing that there's no way out of the pain and despair.

Or perhaps you turn to self-harming as a way to cope with the intense emotional pain you're experiencing. You may engage in behaviors such as cutting, burning, or hitting yourself as a way to numb the emotional turmoil or regain a sense of control over your body.

If no one has ever told you, let me be the one to say it: Narcissistic abusers have mastered the art of making you feel like you're to blame for everything. It's a manipulative tactic designed to keep you under their control, constantly questioning your worth and validity.

When subjected to relentless criticism and manipulation, it's easy to internalize those messages and believe you're somehow to blame for the mistreatment.

In certain relationships, some partners constantly compare their partners to others, pointing out flaws and shortcomings while highlighting the perceived strengths and achievements of those around them. As a victim, you start to believe you're inherently inferior or unworthy, convinced that if only you were smarter, prettier, or more successful, the abuse would stop.

This toxic cycle of comparison and self-blame only perpetuates the abuse and undermines your sense of self-worth. You start to believe you deserve the mistreatment because you're somehow inherently flawed or defective. You may even go so far as to believe that if you were just better in some way, the abuse would magically cease.

Let's say you have a dream or goal you're passionate about—something that lights a fire in your soul and brings you joy. But every time you think about taking steps to pursue it, you're flooded with anxiety and self-doubt. You worry about what the narcissist will say or how they'll react if you dare to step out of line and follow your path.

The fear of doing what you love and achieving success can be paralyzing, trapping you in a cycle of self-sabotage and missed opportunities. You may find yourself holding back, playing small, and settling for less than you deserve because you're afraid of rocking the boat or inviting more criticism and ridicule.

As you read through these signs, perhaps you've experienced some but not others. You might be thinking, "I've faced some bits of narcissistic abuse, but I would never allow myself to experience such and such." It's easy to make such statements until you find yourself in that very situation. Let me share a story with you. A close friend of mine, Milly, took years to realize her narcissistic fiancée was abusing her. Even worse, she found herself defending him. One day, Milly's fiancée lashed out over a trivial matter, berating her with hurtful words and accusations. Instead of recognizing this behavior as abusive, Milly brushed it off, telling herself he was stressed or had a bad day. When her friends expressed concern and pointed out the signs of abuse, Milly defended her fiancée, making excuses for his behavior and down-playing the severity of the situation.

As Milly's story illustrates, it's often challenging to recognize abuse when you're in the midst of it, especially when it comes from someone you love and trust. But part of being trapped in the narcissist's web is defending them, even when it's the last thing either of you deserves. We must be wary of justifying and defending behavior that tears us down instead of lifting us up. It's a reminder that sometimes, the most insidious forms of abuse are the ones we least expect, and it's essential to trust our instincts and seek support when needed.

THE CYCLE OF NARCISSISTIC ABUSE

The thing about narcissistic abuse is that it doesn't appear out of the blue or overnight. Think of it as a seed planted in fertile soil, favored by the right conditions, and allowed to grow into a towering tree. At first, it may seem harmless, even nurturing, but over time, it spreads its roots deep and entangles you in its toxic embrace.

And then this tree bears fruits, scattering its seeds far and wide, each capable of growing into a new tree of narcissistic abuse. The cycle perpetuates itself, spreading its branches of manipulation, control, and toxicity ever further.

The cycle of narcissistic abuse comprises mainly four steps: idealization, devaluation, discard, and re-engagement (Wakefield, 2023). Each step plays a crucial role in perpetuating the cycle and keeping you trapped in the abuser's web of manipulation and control.

During the **idealization phase**, the narcissist creates a fairy tale romance that seems too good to be true. They shower the victim with love, affection, and admiration, painting a picture of perfection and bliss.

Imagine Cassey, a successful and independent woman who meets Adrian at a friend's party. Adrian is charming and attentive and seems genuinely interested in getting to know her. He compliments Cassey on her intelligence, wit, and beauty, making her feel special and appreciated.

As their relationship progresses, Adrian sweeps Cassey off her feet with grand gestures and romantic surprises. He sends her flowers at work, writes her love letters, and plans extravagant dates under the stars. He talks about their future together, painting vivid pictures of travel, adventure, and lifelong companionship.

Cassey is swept away by Adrian's attention and affection. She feels like she's finally found her soulmate, someone who sees her for who she truly is and cherishes her every flaw. In the glow of the idealization phase, Cassey believes she has found true love and happiness.

As they grow fonder of each other, cracks begin to appear in the façade of charm and charisma, signaling the onset of the **devaluation phase.** The narcissist's true colors emerge as their mask starts to slip, and they reveal their capacity for criticism, belittlement, and undermining behavior.

Continuing with Cassey and Adrian's story, as their relationship deepens, Cassey notices subtle changes in Adrian's behavior. He no longer lavishes her with the same level of attention and affection as before. Instead, he starts to criticize her choices, belittle her achievements, and undermine her confidence.

For example, Adrian may scoff at Cassey's career aspirations, dismissing her ambitions as unrealistic or insignificant. He may make cutting remarks about her appearance, subtly implying that she needs to change to meet his beauty standards. He may even gaslight her, making her doubt her perceptions and memories of events.

Adrian's sudden shift in behavior takes Cassey aback. She wonders what she did wrong to deserve his criticism and questions her worth and value in the relationship. Despite her best efforts to please him and regain his approval, Adrian's devaluation tactics continue to erode her self-esteem and confidence.

The devaluation phase is a pivotal moment in the cycle of narcissistic abuse, as it marks the transition from idealization to disillusionment. Cassey is left grappling with feelings of confusion, hurt, and inadequacy as she struggles to make sense of Adrian's sudden change in behavior.

Eventually, after enduring a relentless onslaught of emotional turmoil, the abuse reaches a tipping point, plunging the victim into the harrowing depths of the **discard phase**. In this phase, the narcissist abruptly withdraws their affection and attention, leaving the victim feeling abandoned, confused, and utterly heartbroken. Here's how it unfolds:

In Cassey and Adrian's story, despite Cassey's desperate attempts to salvage their relationship and win back Adrian's approval, she is met with cold indifference and disdain. An icy detachment replaces Adrian's once-charming demeanor as he pulls away, leaving Cassey to wonder what went wrong.

The sudden shift in Adrian's behavior leaves Cassey reeling, struggling to make sense of the whirlwind of emotions coursing through her. She feels as though the ground has been ripped out from under her feet, leaving her adrift in a sea of uncertainty and despair.

As Cassey grapples with feelings of rejection and betrayal, she questions her worth and value. She wonders what she did to deserve such callous treatment and blames herself for failing to meet Adrian's impossible standards.

The discard phase is a profoundly traumatic experience for Cassey as she comes to terms with the devastating reality that the relationship she once cherished was nothing more than an illusion. She is left to pick up the pieces of her shattered heart and rebuild her life from the ground up, knowing she deserves so much more than the crumbs of affection and validation Adrian was willing to offer.

Yet, just when you begin to heal and find the strength to move on, the narcissist may attempt to reel you back in through the cunning tactics of the **re-engagement phase.** In this phase, the narcissist employs various manipulative strategies, such as love bombing or heartfelt apologies, to lure the victim back into the toxic relationship.

In Cassey's case, just as she starts to rebuild her life and rediscover her sense of self-worth, she receives a flurry of messages from Adrian. He bombards her with declarations of love and promises of change, painting a picture of a future filled with happiness and harmony. He begs for another chance, insisting that he has seen the error of his ways and is committed to making things right.

Unsurprisingly, Cassey may find herself tempted to give Adrian another chance despite knowing deep down it may lead her back into the same cycle of narcissistic abuse. The pull of familiarity and the hope for change can be incredibly strong, clouding her judgment and obscuring the red flags that warn of impending danger.

EXAMPLES OF ABUSIVE RELATIONSHIPS

Narcissists are ubiquitous—they can be found in all walks of life, blending seamlessly into our social circles, workplaces, and even our families. They may assume various roles, from the authoritative boss to the charming colleague, the demanding sibling to the controlling parent.

At Work

A while back, I was reading a column on mental health at work, hoping to find some insight into the challenges I had been facing lately. That's when I stumbled upon Calum's story about his narcissistic boss, and suddenly, everything clicked into place.

Let me tell you about it in Calum's own words:

> I never thought I'd find myself in this situation, but here I am, working for the most narcissistic boss you can imagine. At first, I was thrilled to land this job. It seemed like the perfect opportunity to advance my career and make a real impact in the industry.
> But as time went on, I noticed subtle signs that something wasn't right. My boss, let's call him Mr. Smith, had a way of making everything about him. He would take credit for our team's successes, even though he had little to do with them and deflect blame onto us when things went wrong.
> I remember one instance where I spent weeks working on a project, pouring my heart and soul into it, only for Mr. Smith to swoop in at the last minute and present it as his own idea. He didn't even

acknowledge my contribution, let alone thank me for my hard work.

But it wasn't just about stealing credit. Mr. Smith had a knack for undermining my confidence and making me doubt myself at every turn. He would nitpick every little detail of my work, pointing out flaws that weren't even there and tearing down my ideas without offering any constructive feedback.

I felt like I was walking on eggshells every day, afraid to speak up or assert myself out of fear of retaliation. It was like being trapped in a toxic cycle of manipulation and control with no way out.

Eventually, I realized I couldn't continue working in such a toxic environment. I made the difficult decision to leave the company, even though it meant sacrificing the stability and security of my job. But in the end, my mental health and well-being were more important than any paycheck.

Calum's story struck a chord with me because it echoed many of the challenges I'd faced in my workplace. It was reassuring to know I was not alone in dealing with narcissistic bosses and that there was hope for a better, healthier work environment.

Family

Some narcissists are the products of childhood trauma. They were raised in families where narcissistic abuse was the order of the day. Michaela, an acquaintance of mine, bravely shared her ordeal of growing up with a narcissistic half-brother. Here's her story in her own words:

I never really understood the term "narcissistic abuse" until I found myself living it day in and day out under the same roof as my half-brother. From the outside, our family seemed picture-perfect, but behind closed doors, it was a different story entirely.

My half-brother, Jake, was the golden child in my father's eyes. He could do no wrong, and my father doted on him endlessly, showering him with praise and attention while neglecting me and my siblings.

From a young age, I was subjected to Jake's cruel and manipulative behavior. He would gaslight me, making me doubt my own memories and perceptions of reality. He would steal my belongings and blame me for his own mistakes, leaving me feeling confused and powerless.

But perhaps the most insidious form of abuse was emotional manipulation. Jake had a way of twisting situations to make himself the victim, turning my own family against me and leaving me isolated and alone.

I remember one incident vividly when Jake spread vicious rumors about me to our extended family, painting me as the villain and himself as the innocent victim. I was devastated and felt completely betrayed by the brother I had once looked up to.

Living with a narcissistic family member took a toll on my self-esteem. I struggled with feelings of worthlessness and inadequacy, constantly seeking validation and approval from others to fill the void left by Jake's emotional abuse.

Friendships

I could be wrong, but I bet most of us have had an experience with a narcissistic friend. I certainly did during my college years. Let me share my story about Aaliyah, a friend who left a lasting impact on me.

College was supposed to be a time of growth, exploration, and forging lifelong friendships. And for the most part, it was. But then there was Aaliyah.

At first, Aaliyah seemed like the perfect friend. She was charismatic and outgoing, and she was always the life of the party. We hit it off right away, bonding over shared interests and aspirations. But as our friendship progressed, I noticed subtle signs that something wasn't quite right.

Aaliyah had a way of making everything about her. She monopolized conversations, constantly steering them back to her experiences and achievements. She seemed to thrive on validation and attention, always seeking praise and admiration from those around her.

I remember one incident when I shared some exciting news with Aaliyah, expecting her to be happy for me. Instead, she immediately shifted the focus back to herself, downplaying my accomplishments and belittling them. I felt deflated and invalidated as if my successes didn't matter compared to hers.

But perhaps the most troubling aspect of our friendship was Aaliyah's habit of using me as a pawn in her social games. She would manipulate situations to her advantage, using me to gain access to certain social circles or further her agenda. I felt like I was being used and discarded at her convenience, with no regard for my feelings or well-being.

Despite my growing discomfort with our friendship, I found myself reluctant to confront Aaliyah or set boundaries. I was afraid of rocking the boat or risking conflict, so I tolerated her behavior in silence.

INSIDE THE MIND OF AN ABUSER

Have you ever laid back and asked yourself, "Why do narcissists do whatever they do?" It's a question that has puzzled many of us who have encountered narcissistic behavior in our lives. Understanding the mindset of the abuser can shed light on their motivations and help us make sense of their actions.

For narcissists, maintaining a façade of perfection and control is paramount. They see themselves as superior beings, entitled to special treatment and admiration from those around them. Any perceived threat to their ego or self-image is met with defensiveness, aggression, or manipulation. Think about a family member who constantly criticizes others and deflects blame onto them to avoid facing their shortcomings. Their behavior is driven by a need to protect their fragile ego and maintain their sense of superiority. By shifting responsibility onto others, they shield themselves from scrutiny and maintain the illusion of perfection, even at the expense of hurting those closest to them.

At the heart of narcissistic behavior is a profound fear of rejection and abandonment. Narcissists are terrified of being exposed as frauds or unworthy of love and admiration. To protect themselves from this perceived threat, they resort to tactics such as gaslighting, manipulation, and emotional abuse to maintain power and control over others.

But beneath the bravado lies a deep well of insecurity and self-loathing. Narcissists may project an image of confidence and self-assuredness, but in reality, they are plagued by feelings of emptiness and inadequacy. Their behavior is driven by a desperate need for validation and approval, which they seek to fulfill through manipulating and exploiting others.

It's worth knowing that some narcissists suffer from narcissistic vulnerability. Think about a boss who reacts with hostility and defensiveness to any perceived criticism or challenge to their authority. Under their façade of confidence lies a deep-seated vulnerability, driving them to lash out at others to protect themselves from feelings of insecurity and inadequacy. Their narcissistic vulnerability manifests as aggression and hostility toward those who threaten their fragile egos.

Additionally, narcissists tend to overlook **boundaries**. Think of a sibling who consistently oversteps boundaries and disregards the autonomy and needs of others. Their lack of boundaries stems from the belief that they are entitled to intrude on the lives and spaces of others without consequence. Their narcissistic lack of boundaries leads to toxic dynamics in their relationships, as they fail to respect the personal boundaries and autonomy of those around them.

A major complex that narcissists deal with is denial. Imagine a colleague who refuses to acknowledge their role in perpetuating toxic dynamics in the workplace. Despite evidence to the contrary, they deny any wrongdoing or responsibility for their actions, shifting blame onto others instead. Their narcissistic denial prevents them from taking accountability for their behavior and seeking meaningful change, contributing to a toxic work environment.

We could go on and on about why narcissists are that way, but we must agree that, in many ways, narcissists are prisoners of their minds, trapped in a cycle of toxic behavior that ultimately leaves them isolated and unfulfilled. While their actions may cause harm to those around them, it's essential to recognize that narcissists are ultimately victims of their own inner turmoil and psychological wounds.

Nonetheless, it does not mean that we tolerate the abuse they expose us to. While understanding the roots of narcissistic behavior can evoke empathy and compassion, it doesn't excuse or justify the harm they inflict on others. It's essential to prioritize our own mental and emotional health and take proactive steps to distance ourselves from harmful relationships. While we can offer support and understanding to those struggling with narcissistic tendencies, we must also prioritize our safety and well-being above all else.

IT'S NOT YOUR FAULT

Let's clear something up: The abuse you've endured is absolutely not your fault. Seriously, not even a little bit. It's crucial to understand that the responsibility for abusive behavior lies solely with the abuser.

Think about it this way: Just because someone decides to mistreat you doesn't mean you asked for it or deserved it in any way. Abuse is a deliberate choice made by the abuser, driven by their insecurities, control issues, and lack of empathy.

You're not responsible for someone else's actions or their inability to treat you with the respect and kindness you deserve. You didn't cause their abusive behavior, and you certainly can't control it.

It's also important to recognize that abusers often manipulate their victims into believing they're to blame for the abuse. They'll twist things around, gaslight you, and make you doubt yourself. But let me tell you loud and clear: You are not to blame.

No matter what the abuser says or does, you have the right to be treated with dignity, respect, and kindness. You deserve to feel safe and valued in your relationships, and anyone who can't provide that doesn't deserve a place in your life.

So, repeat after me: "It's not my fault." Say it as many times as you need to until it sinks in.

ARE YOU BEING ABUSED?

As you go through this checklist, refer back to the scenarios and examples discussed above. These real-life situations can provide valuable insights into the themes and patterns of narcissistic abuse. Take time to reflect on your experiences, and don't hesitate to reach out for support if needed.

Take a moment to reflect on each question and answer honestly with a simple yes or no. Remember, this checklist is meant to help you gain clarity and insight into your relationship dynamics. If you find yourself answering yes to multiple questions, it may be a sign that you're experiencing abuse from a narcissistic partner.

1. Does your partner frequently criticize or belittle you, making you feel small or inadequate?
2. Do you often feel like you're walking on eggshells around your partner, afraid to say or do anything that might upset them?
3. Have you sacrificed your needs and desires to cater to your partner's demands and expectations?
4. Are you experiencing physical or emotional health issues as a result of the stress and turmoil in your relationship?
5. Do you find yourself mistrusting your thoughts and feelings, constantly second-guessing yourself?
6. Have you ever experienced thoughts of self-harm or suicide due to the abuse you're enduring?
7. Do you frequently compare yourself to others, feeling like you're always falling short or not good enough?
8. Are you afraid to pursue your passions and goals, fearing your partner's disapproval or sabotage?
9. Do you often find yourself defending or justifying your partner's abusive behavior to others?
10. Have you ever felt trapped or unable to leave the relationship despite knowing it's unhealthy for you?

As we channel into Chapter 2, get ready to break free from the toxic grip of manipulation and codependency and discover empowering strategies to release yourself from the chains that bind you to unhealthy relationships. It's time to reclaim your independence and rediscover your inner strength. You can take back control of your life and chart a path toward healing and liberation.

R—RELEASE YOURSELF FROM THE CHAINS OF MANIPULATION AND CODEPENDENCY

"You don't let go of a bad relationship because you stop caring about them. You let go because you started caring about yourself."

CHARLES ORLANDO

I have known Christy for as long as I can remember and had never seen her in this position. She was always the confident, vibrant soul who seemed to effortlessly navigate life's challenges with grace and resilience. But as I sat across from her, watching the flicker of uncertainty in her eyes, I realized something had changed.

Christy began to open up about her relationship, which had left her feeling broken and powerless. For years, she had been caught in a web of manipulation and gaslighting, her every thought and feeling twisted and distorted by her partner's relentless tactics. Slowly but surely, Christy's sense of self had been eroded, leaving behind a shell of the person she once was.

As she spoke, it became painfully clear just how deeply the scars of manipulation and codependency ran. Christy questioned her worth, doubted her instincts, and struggled to assert herself in even the simplest of situations. The damage inflicted by her toxic relationship had seeped into every aspect of her life, leaving her feeling trapped and powerless.

But as Christy shared her story, I could see a glimmer of hope flickering beneath the surface. She was tired of living in the shadow of her abuser and of allowing her past to dictate her future. And that's where this chapter comes in.

In Chapter 2, we'll explore the insidious nature of manipulation and codependency, shining a light on the tactics used by abusers to maintain control over their victims. But more importantly, we'll discuss strategies for breaking free from these chains and reclaiming your sense of self-worth and agency.

BEATING MANIPULATION

Manipulation is when someone tries to control or influence you sneakily or deceptively, often to get what they want or to make you do something you wouldn't normally do. It can take many forms, from subtle persuasion to outright deception, and it often involves playing on your emotions or exploiting your vulnerabilities.

For example, imagine a friend who always seems to get their way by making you feel guilty whenever you disagree with them. They might say things like, "I thought you were my friend, but I guess I was wrong," or "If you really cared about me, you would do this for me." Without realizing it, you start to feel bad for standing up for yourself and end up giving in to their demands.

Manipulation can also involve lying or distorting the truth to get what someone wants. For instance, a coworker might spread rumors about you to undermine your reputation and advance their agenda at work. Or a romantic partner might downplay their past behavior or make false promises to keep you from leaving the relationship.

Quite often, we may not realize we are being manipulated. We might think we're just being kind or accommodating, but in reality, we're falling victim to someone else's subtle tactics. Here are five questions to ask yourself to know if you're being manipulated:

1. Do you often feel guilty or ashamed for setting boundaries or saying no to someone? Manipulative people are skilled at making you feel responsible for their feelings, even when you've done nothing wrong.
2. Are you constantly second-guessing your thoughts, feelings, or decisions? Manipulators often undermine your confidence and judgment, making you doubt yourself and rely on them for validation.
3. Do you feel like you owe someone something, even if they haven't explicitly asked for it? Manipulators may use guilt or obligation to pressure you into doing things you don't want to do.
4. Have you noticed changes in your behavior, such as avoiding certain topics or activities to avoid conflict? Manipulators may use fear or intimidation to control your actions and keep you in line.

5. Do you feel emotionally drained or exhausted after interacting with someone? Manipulative people often leave you feeling depleted after encounters, as they drain your energy and emotional resources.

What Next?

Imagine you're having a conversation with a friend who always seems to steer the discussion toward their interests and dismiss your opinions. They constantly interrupt you, change the subject whenever it's not about them, and make you feel like your thoughts and feelings don't matter.

It can be challenging to know how to respond to this manipulation in the moment. You might feel tempted to go along with their behavior to avoid conflict or keep the peace. But standing up for yourself is crucial for maintaining healthy boundaries and preserving your self-respect.

Here's what you could do in that scenario:

1. **Recognize the manipulation.** Take a moment to step back and recognize what's happening. Acknowledge that your friend is attempting to manipulate the conversation to serve their agenda.
2. **Stay calm.** It's essential to remain calm and composed, even if you feel frustrated or angry. Responding with emotion may escalate the situation and give the manipulator more power over you.
3. **Set boundaries.** Assert yourself by setting clear boundaries about what behavior is acceptable to you. You could say something like, "I understand you have a lot on your mind, but I'd appreciate it if

we could take turns talking and listening to each other."

4. **Redirect the conversation.** If the manipulation continues, gently redirect the conversation to a topic that interests you or that you feel comfortable discussing. Don't allow the manipulator to dictate the direction of the conversation.

5. **Take a break if necessary.** If the manipulation persists and you feel overwhelmed, taking a break from the interaction is okay. Politely excuse yourself from the conversation and give yourself time to regroup and collect your thoughts.

How to Regain Your Power and Heal From Manipulation

Manipulation is often not a one-time event; it can leave long-term effects on our mental and emotional well-being. However, it's crucial to recognize that even in the aftermath of manipulation and abuse, you haven't lost your power. You still can regain control over your life and heal from the wounds inflicted by manipulative individuals.

In your journey to overcome manipulative abuse, you may have encountered numerous pieces of advice and strategies aimed at helping you regain control of your life. While many of these strategies are undoubtedly valuable, knowing your triggers is a crucial aspect I've found particularly impactful in my experiences.

Imagine you're at work, and your supervisor calls you into their office for a performance review. As you sit across from them, you can feel your heart racing and your palms starting to sweat. Despite your best efforts to stay calm and composed, you can't shake the feeling of dread that washes over you every time you're called into their office.

As your supervisor begins to critique your work, pointing out perceived flaws and areas for improvement, you feel a familiar sense of insecurity and self-doubt creeping in. You find yourself nodding along, unable to speak up or defend yourself, even when you know their criticisms are unjustified.

After the meeting ends, you retreat to your desk, feeling defeated and demoralized. You replay the conversation in your mind, analyzing every word and action, wondering what you could have done differently to avoid feeling so powerless and vulnerable.

In this scenario, the performance review triggers feelings of vulnerability and powerlessness rooted in past experiences of criticism or rejection. Despite your best efforts to stay grounded and assertive, you succumb to the same patterns of self-doubt and compliance that have plagued you in the past.

By identifying this trigger and understanding its origins, you can gain insight into the specific situations or circumstances that leave you susceptible to manipulation and abuse in the workplace.

Identifying triggers is just the first step—the real work begins when we take proactive measures to address and mitigate their impact on our lives. Setting boundaries is crucial in safeguarding our emotional well-being and protecting ourselves from manipulation and abuse. By clearly defining what behaviors and treatments we will not tolerate, we establish a line that others cannot cross without consequence.

Having an exit plan is paramount to fully regaining your power and breaking free from a manipulative relationship. It provides a roadmap for safely extricating yourself from the toxic dynamics and reclaiming control over your life. Here's what an exit plan may entail:

- Begin by assessing your safety and well-being. Consider any potential risks or threats posed by the manipulative individual and prioritize your physical and emotional safety above all else.
- Reach out to trusted friends, family members, or support networks who can offer guidance, assistance, and emotional support during this challenging time. A strong support system can provide invaluable encouragement and resources as you navigate the exit process.
- Take steps to establish financial independence and autonomy, if possible. This may involve securing employment, opening a separate bank account, or seeking financial assistance from community resources or organizations dedicated to supporting survivors of abuse.
- Document any instances of manipulation, coercion, or abuse you have experienced. Keep a detailed record of relevant communications, incidents, and interactions, including dates, times, and descriptions of events. This documentation can serve as crucial evidence if legal action or intervention becomes necessary.

- Consider seeking support from mental health professionals, counselors, or therapists who specialize in trauma and abuse recovery. Therapy can provide a safe space to process your experiences, gain insights into patterns of manipulation, and develop coping strategies for healing and moving forward.
- Once your exit plan is in place, take decisive action to implement it. This may involve ending contact with the manipulative individual, leaving the shared living space, and protecting your personal belongings and assets. Trust your instincts and prioritize your well-being as you take the necessary steps to break free from the abusive relationship.

OVERCOMING CODEPENDENCY

A great number of us deal with codependency. It's a silent struggle that often goes unnoticed, yet it shapes our relationships and profoundly influences our behaviors.

But what exactly is codependency?

Codependency is a complex and deeply ingrained pattern of behavior characterized by excessive reliance on others for validation, approval, and a sense of identity. It often manifests in relationships where one person consistently prioritizes the needs and desires of their partner above their own, sacrificing their well-being in the process. Codependents may struggle with boundary-setting, struggle with low self-esteem, and have difficulty asserting their own needs and desires.

Like many of us, Penny, a friend I met in one of the self-help communities, was a victim of narcissistic abuse stemming from codependency; she was deeply entrenched in a toxic relationship with Joe. Penny is a compassionate and caring woman who always puts others' needs before her own. She's been in a relationship with Joe for several years, and although she loves him deeply, their relationship is far from healthy.

Joe is charismatic and charming but also manipulative and emotionally distant. He's a classic narcissist, constantly seeking validation and admiration from others while dismissing or belittling Penny's feelings and needs. Despite his flaws, Penny remains devoted to him, convinced that she can fix him and make their relationship work.

In their relationship, Penny constantly finds herself bending over backward to accommodate Joe's ever-changing demands and mood swings. She sacrifices her happiness and well-being to keep the peace and avoid conflict. She tolerates his controlling behavior, rationalizing it as a sign of his love and concern for her.

Meanwhile, Joe exploits Penny's unwavering loyalty and devotion to fulfill his needs and desires. He manipulates her with guilt trips and emotional blackmail, using her codependency to maintain control over her and keep her trapped in the relationship.

Despite the toxicity of their dynamic, Penny struggles to break free from the cycle of codependency and narcissistic abuse. She fears being alone and worries about what others will think if she leaves Joe. She clings to the hope that he'll change and become the loving partner she yearns for, ignoring the red flags and warning signs that indicate otherwise.

In this story, Penny's codependency enables Joe's narcissistic behavior to thrive, perpetuating a cycle of dysfunction and unhappiness. It's a painful and all-too-common scenario that many of us can relate to, highlighting the insidious nature of codependency and the detrimental impact it can have on relationships.

Nonetheless, it's important to understand that regardless of whether you suffer from codependency, it's not a guarantee that you should be subjected to narcissistic abuse. It's never your fault, and it's a choice that your abuser makes. Recognizing this is a crucial step toward breaking free from the cycle of abuse and reclaiming your power and autonomy.

Stages of Codependency

Let's talk about the stages of codependency. Codependency can manifest in different stages, progressing from early to middle to late stages. Interestingly, the level of narcissistic abuse you endure may correspond to your level of codependency. As your codependency deepens, you may become more enmeshed in the dynamics of the abusive relationship, making it increasingly challenging to break free.

To understand the stages of codependency, let's engage with Kayla's story. Kayla, a bright and ambitious young woman, landed her dream job at a prestigious company right out of college. Full of enthusiasm and determination, she poured her heart and soul into her work, often going above and beyond what was expected. Here is the story in her own words:

Let me tell you about my experience with codependency at work. When I first started my job, I was so excited. I loved what I did, and I was eager to prove myself. My boss, Mr. Thompson, seemed really impressed with my work ethic and dedication. He praised me all the time, and it felt amazing to be recognized for my efforts.

But things started to change. Mr. Thompson started giving me more and more responsibilities without any extra support. At first, I didn't mind—I wanted to show him I could handle anything he threw at me. But soon, it became too much. I was working late nights and weekends and felt like I was drowning in work.

I wanted to speak up and tell Mr. Thompson that I needed help, but I was afraid. I didn't want to disappoint him or seem weak. So, I just kept pushing myself harder and harder, hoping that things would get better.

As time went on, things only got worse. Mr. Thompson's demands became even more unreasonable, and he started taking advantage of my willingness to please him.

But instead of standing up for myself, I bent over backward to meet his impossible standards. I was afraid of losing my job or disappointing him, so I just kept pushing myself harder and harder, hoping that things would eventually get better.

But they never did. The more I tried to please Mr. Thompson, the more he exploited my codependency. He manipulated me with promises of promotions or raises, only to pull the rug out from under me at the last minute. He would gaslight me, making me doubt my own abilities and sanity.

I was stuck in a never-ending cycle of trying to earn Mr. Thompson's approval, even though, deep down, I knew it was impossible. I felt trapped and helpless like I had no way out.

My codependency had made me even more vulnerable to Mr. Thompson's manipulation and abuse. I was so deeply enmeshed in the toxic dynamic that I couldn't see a way out.

Mr. Thompson's behavior became increasingly erratic and abusive. He would fly into fits of rage over minor mistakes, shouting and berating me in front of my colleagues. He would withhold praise and recognition, making me feel worthless and unappreciated. And yet, despite his cruelty, I couldn't bring myself to leave.

I had become completely dependent on Mr. Thompson for validation and approval. I had lost all sense of self-worth and identity outside of my job. I was consumed by fear and self-doubt, convinced I was powerless to change my situation.

But deep down, I knew I couldn't continue living like this. I couldn't allow myself to be a victim of Mr. Thompson's abuse any longer. I had to find the strength within myself to break free from his grip and reclaim my autonomy.

It wasn't easy. It took a lot of courage and determination to finally stand up to Mr. Thompson and walk away from the toxic environment he had created. But in the end, it was worth it. I may have been a victim of narcissistic abuse, but I refused to let it define me. I

was determined to heal and rebuild my life on my
own terms.

Kayla's journey through the three stages of codependency offers a poignant illustration of the progression from early dependence to full-scale entrapment in a toxic relationship. In the early stage, she was drawn to Mr. Thompson's charisma and charm, eager to please him and gain his approval. As the middle stage unfolded, she became increasingly enmeshed in the cycle of manipulation and abuse, her sense of self-worth diminishing with each passing day. Finally, in the third stage, Kayla reached a breaking point, realizing she could no longer tolerate Mr. Thompson's toxic behavior and taking decisive action to break free from his control.

Are You Codependent?

I understand that recognizing codependency and narcissistic abuse can be challenging, especially when you're in the midst of it. To help you gain insight into your situation, here's a simple checklist for you to consider.

1. Do you often prioritize other people's needs and desires over your own?
2. Do you feel responsible for other people's emotions and well-being?
3. Do you have difficulty saying no, even when it's not in your best interest?
4. Do you often feel guilty or anxious when setting boundaries with others?
5. Do you find yourself constantly seeking approval and validation from others?

6. Do you struggle with low self-esteem and self-worth?
7. Do you have a history of being in relationships where you felt taken advantage of or exploited?
8. Do you avoid conflict at all costs, even if it means sacrificing your needs?
9. Do you have difficulty expressing your thoughts, feelings, and opinions openly and honestly?
10. Do you feel you need to "fix" or rescue others from their problems, even if it negatively impacts your well-being?

How to Break Free from Codependency

Kayla shared that deciding to reclaim her independence, restore her power, and overcome the narcissistic abuse Mr. Thompson had subjected her to was the best decision she ever made. Yet, it wasn't as straightforward as it may sound. She had to navigate through layers of emotional turmoil, self-doubt, and fear before she could break free from the chains of codependency.

Breaking free from codependency typically involves four crucial steps that Kayla discovered on her journey to healing and independence. Each step is a building block toward reclaiming one's sense of self-worth and autonomy despite the challenges that may arise along the way.

Step 1: Become aware of your codependent habits and be curious about who you really are.

The first step in breaking free from codependency is to shine a light on the patterns and behaviors that have kept you tethered to unhealthy relationships. It's about acknowledging that your self-worth and identity have become entangled with others, often to your detriment. When you recognize these codependent habits, you can start unraveling the complex web that has kept you bound to the needs and desires of others.

But awareness is just the beginning. It's also about cultivating a sense of curiosity about who you truly are beneath the layers of codependency. This means exploring your needs, desires, and values independently of anyone else's expectations or validation. It's about rediscovering your strengths, passions, and dreams that may have been over-shadowed by your focus on others.

For Kayla, this meant taking a step back and reflecting on how she had prioritized Mr. Thompson's needs over hers. She began to notice the patterns of people-pleasing and self-sacrifice that had become second nature to her. With each moment of awareness, she gained a deeper understanding of how her codependent habits had shaped her relationships and her sense of self.

Step 2: Set boundaries.

After Kayla's realization of her codependency and the toxic dynamics in her relationship with Mr. Thompson, she knew she had to set boundaries to break free. She started by clearly defining her limits and identifying the behaviors detrimental to her well-being.

For instance, she made a conscious decision to no longer tolerate Mr. Thompson's manipulation and emotional abuse. She set boundaries around her time and energy, refusing to engage in conversations or activities that left her feeling drained or invalidated. Kayla also learned to say no to unreasonable demands and assert her needs and preferences without fear of reprisal.

In addition to setting boundaries with Mr. Thompson, Kayla also established boundaries with herself. She recognized the importance of self-care and made it a priority in her daily life. This included setting aside time for activities that brought her joy and relaxation, such as painting, journaling, and spending time with supportive friends.

Step 3: Practice self-compassion and self-acceptance.

After setting boundaries, the next step in breaking free from codependency is to practice self-compassion and self-acceptance. This involves learning to treat yourself with kindness, understanding, and forgiveness, especially in moments of struggle or setback.

For Kayla, practicing self-compassion was a crucial part of her healing journey. She realized she had spent so much time criticizing and blaming herself for the dysfunction in her relationship with Mr. Thompson. However, she came to understand that she was not to blame for his abusive behavior.

Instead of berating herself for staying in the relationship for so long or for not recognizing the signs of abuse sooner, Kayla learned to show herself the same compassion and empathy she would extend to a friend in a similar situation. She acknowledged her worth and inherent value, regardless of her past mistakes or shortcomings.

In addition to self-compassion, Kayla also embraced self-acceptance. She recognized that she was imperfect and flawed, like everyone else, and that having her own unique set of strengths and weaknesses was okay. By accepting herself fully, flaws and all, Kayla found the courage to let go of the need for external validation and approval.

Step 4: Seek support and professional help.

The final step in breaking free from codependency is to seek support and professional help when needed. This involves reaching out to trusted friends, family members, support groups, or therapists who can offer guidance, encouragement, and perspective as you navigate your healing journey.

Initially, Kayla felt ashamed and embarrassed to admit the extent of her struggles with codependency and narcissistic abuse. However, she eventually found the courage to confide in a close friend, who offered unwavering support and validation.

With her friend's encouragement, Kayla began attending therapy sessions with a licensed counselor who specialized in trauma and relationship issues. Through therapy, she gained valuable insights into her codependent patterns and learned practical strategies for setting boundaries, building self-esteem, and processing her emotions.

In addition to therapy, Kayla also found solace in online support groups and self-help resources dedicated to survivors of narcissistic abuse and codependency. Connecting with others with similar experiences helped her feel less alone and gave her a sense of community and validation.

It's important to recognize that the journey to breaking free from codependency and healing from narcissistic abuse is unique for each individual. While some may make significant progress relatively quickly, others may require more time and patience to fully overcome these challenges.

Regardless of the timeline, what matters most is having the determination and willingness to regain your power and prioritize your healing journey. It's okay to take things one step at a time and seek support whenever needed along the way.

Healing is not always linear, and there may be setbacks or obstacles along the way. But with perseverance, self-compassion, and a commitment to your own well-being, you can overcome codependency and reclaim your sense of self-worth and autonomy.

In Chapter 3, we focus on the crucial steps to safely escape the traps set by narcissists.

E—ESCAPE THE NARCISSIST'S TRAPS SAFELY

"When we meet and fall into the gravitational pull of a narcissist, we are entering a significant life lesson that involves learning how to create boundaries, self-respect, and resilience. Through trial and error (and a lot of pain), our connection with narcissists teaches us the necessary lessons we need to become mature empaths."

MATEO SOL

Each time I think of how hard it can be to leave a narcissist, Caitlyn's story comes to mind. Here is Caitlyn sharing her experience in her own words:

It's like I was trapped in a maze with no way out. Every time I tried to leave, he would reel me back in with promises of change and apologies that I desperately wanted to believe. But deep down, I knew it was just a cycle—a vicious cycle of manipulation and control that kept me bound to him. I felt suffocated, drowning in a sea of uncertainty and fear.

Caitlyn's story is just one of countless others who have found themselves trapped in the web of a narcissistic relationship. The emotional turmoil, the gaslighting, the constant roller-coaster of highs and lows—it's enough to make anyone feel like they're losing their grip on reality.

But there is hope. In this chapter, we'll explore strategies and techniques to help you safely escape the traps set by narcissists.

SIGNS A NARCISSIST IS "DISCARDING" YOU

To escape a narcissist's traps, you must recognize when they are discarding you. This phase can be one of the most painful and confusing parts of a narcissistic relationship, as the narcissist abruptly withdraws their affection and attention, leaving you feeling abandoned and discarded.

One sign that a narcissist is discarding you is when they start to emotionally and physically withdraw from the relationship. They may become distant, cold, and indifferent toward you, no longer showing the same level of affection or interest as they did before. For example, they might stop responding to your calls or texts, cancel plans at the last minute, or avoid spending time with you altogether.

Usually, the narcissist starts to devalue and criticize you more frequently. They may nitpick everything you do, undermine your achievements, and make you feel inade-quate or worthless. For instance, they might mock your appearance, intelligence, or accomplishments, leaving you feeling insecure and unworthy of their love and attention.

The narcissist may also start to idealize someone else, such as a new romantic interest or a friend, while simultaneously devaluing and discarding you. They may flaunt their new relationship or friendship in front of you, making you feel jealous, insecure, and insignificant in comparison.

In extreme cases, the narcissist may discard you abruptly and without warning, leaving you shocked and devastated. They may end the relationship callously and cruelly, blaming you for everything that went wrong and refusing to take responsibility for their actions.

Understanding why a narcissist will discard you is crucial for your healing journey. It's not because of anything you did or didn't do; it's about them and their internal struggles. Ian's story sheds light on this painful aspect of narcissistic relationships.

Ian was in a relationship with a narcissistic partner for years, and despite his unwavering love and devotion, he found himself discarded without warning. At first, Ian blamed himself, wondering what he did wrong to deserve such treatment. But as he embarked on his healing journey, he came to realize that the discard was not about him—it was about his partner's inability to maintain a genuine connection.

Narcissists discard their partners for several reasons, but one of the main ones is their insatiable need for validation and admiration. They are constantly seeking new sources of narcissistic supply to fuel their fragile egos, and once they perceive that you no longer serve that purpose, they move on to someone else who can fulfill their needs.

Additionally, narcissists lack empathy and are unable to form deep and meaningful connections with others. They see people as objects to be used for their benefit, and once they've drained you of your energy and resources, they discard you without a second thought.

Furthermore, narcissists are driven by a fear of abandonment and rejection. They discard their partners preemptively to avoid being rejected themselves, even if it means causing immense pain and suffering to the ones they claim to love.

In Ian's case, his partner discarded him because she found someone new who could give her the attention and validation she craved. It wasn't because Ian wasn't good enough or deserving of love; it was because his partner was incapable of forming genuine connections and maintaining healthy relationships.

Understanding why a narcissist will discard you can be painful, but it's an essential part of the healing process. It allows you to let go of any lingering doubts or self-blame and recognize that the discard was never about you—it was about the narcissist's insecurities and shortcomings.

What to Expect after a Discard

After experiencing a discard from a narcissistic partner, it's natural to feel a whirlwind of emotions and uncertainties. You may be left reeling from the abrupt end of the relationship and grappling with a sense of loss and betrayal.

First and foremost, it's important to acknowledge that the aftermath of a discard can be incredibly challenging. You may find yourself experiencing a range of emotions, from sadness and anger to confusion and self-doubt. These feelings are valid and normal reactions to such a traumatic event, and it's essential to give yourself permission to process them in your own time and way.

One of the most common experiences after a discard is a sense of disbelief and shock. You may struggle to come to terms with the sudden end of the relationship and find yourself questioning what went wrong. It's natural to search for answers and try to make sense of the situation, but it's important to recognize that closure may not come easily, especially when dealing with a narcissistic partner who lacks empathy and transparency.

Narcissistic partners often undermine their victims' self-esteem and confidence through manipulation and gaslighting, leaving them feeling unworthy and inadequate. In the aftermath of a discard, you may find yourself grappling with feelings of worthlessness and self-doubt, wondering if you'll ever be able to trust yourself or others again.

Additionally, you may experience a sense of social isolation and withdrawal after a discard. Narcissistic partners often isolate their victims from friends and family members, leaving them feeling alone and disconnected from their support networks. As you navigate life after the discard, you may find yourself rebuilding relationships and reconnecting with loved ones who can provide you with the support and validation you need.

WHEN YOU HAVEN'T BEEN "DISCARDED": SIGNS IT'S TIME TO LEAVE YOUR NARCISSISTIC RELATIONSHIP

Indeed, sometimes, a narcissistic abuser won't discard you but instead keeps you around to continue the cycle of abuse. In such situations, it's crucial to recognize the signs that it's time to leave the relationship for your well-being. Let's proceed with Caitlyn's story and allow her to share the signs that ultimately pushed her to leave her narcissistic relationship.

> I remember feeling trapped in a never-ending cycle of manipulation and control. At first, I brushed off the subtle signs of abuse, convincing myself that things would get better. But as time went on, the signs became harder to ignore.

Caitlyn recalls feeling constantly on edge, walking on eggshells to avoid setting off her partner's anger. "I found myself tiptoeing around their moods and constantly second-guessing my every move. It felt like I was living in a constant state of fear and anxiety, never knowing when the next outburst would occur."

Another sign that pushed Caitlyn to leave was the erosion of her self-esteem and confidence. "I used to be a strong, independent person, but over time, my partner's constant criticism and belittling wore me down. I started to doubt myself and my worth, convinced that I was the one at fault for everything that went wrong in the relationship."

Additionally, Caitlyn recalls feeling isolated and alone, cut off from friends and family members who could offer support and validation. "My partner made me believe they were the only ones who truly cared about me, isolating me from anyone who might challenge their control over me. It wasn't until I reached out to a trusted friend for help that I realized just how toxic and unhealthy the relationship had become."

Ultimately, it was a combination of these signs, along with Caitlyn's inner strength and resilience, that prompted her to leave her narcissistic relationship. "Leaving wasn't easy, and I had to confront my fears and insecurities head-on. But looking back, I know it was the best decision I ever made for myself."

Caitlyn's story serves as a reminder that sometimes the signs to leave a narcissistic relationship may not be obvious at first, but they are there if you're willing to see them. If you find yourself experiencing similar feelings of fear, isolation, and self-doubt, it may be time to reevaluate the relationship and prioritize your well-being.

STEP-BY-STEP PROCESS TO SAFELY LEAVE A NARCISSIST

Leaving a narcissist can be an incredibly challenging and daunting task, but it's also a crucial step toward reclaiming your life and well-being. While there's no one-size-fits-all blueprint for how to leave, following a step-by-step process can help you navigate the journey from abuse to freedom and peace of mind.

1. **Understand why it can be hard to leave.** Recognize that leaving a narcissistic relationship can be difficult due to various factors such as fear, guilt,

manipulation, and financial dependence. It's important to acknowledge and validate your feelings while also understanding you deserve to live a life free from abuse.

2. **Create a plan and be prepared.** Before taking any steps toward leaving, create a safety plan and consider all possible scenarios. This may include securing a safe place to stay, gathering important documents, and reaching out to trusted friends or family members for support. A well-thought-out plan can help you feel more empowered and prepared for the journey ahead.

3. **Don't tell the narcissist you're planning on leaving.** While it may be tempting to confront the narcissist and announce your intentions to leave, doing so can put you at risk of further manipulation, abuse, or retaliation. Instead, focus on quietly and discreetly making your exit plan without alerting the narcissist to your intentions.

4. **Set aside some spare cash.** Financial independence is key to safely leaving a narcissistic relationship. Start setting aside some spare cash in a secret account or safe place where the narcissist can't access it. Having financial resources available can provide you with the freedom and flexibility to make your escape when the time comes.

5. **Check your digital trail.** Be mindful of your online activity and digital footprint, as narcissists may try to monitor or track your movements. Delete any incriminating or sensitive information from your devices, change passwords to secure accounts, and

consider using a secure communication method when reaching out for help or support.

6. **Side with yourself.** In the midst of a narcissistic relationship, it's common to feel like you're constantly walking on eggshells or prioritizing the narcissist's needs over your own. As you prepare to leave, remember to prioritize yourself and your well-being above all else. Make decisions in your best interest and focus on your needs and desires.

7. **Discreetly let others know and build a support system.** Reach out to trusted friends, family members, or support groups, and discreetly let them know about your situation. Building a support system of understanding and empathetic individuals can provide you with emotional support, validation, and practical assistance as you navigate the challenges of leaving a narcissistic relationship.

8. **Seek professional support.** Consider seeking guidance from a therapist, counselor, or support group specializing in narcissistic abuse and domestic violence. A trained professional can offer you valuable insights, coping strategies, and emotional support as you work through the complexities of leaving and healing from the abuse.

9. **Go no-contact, and do it cold turkey.** Once you've decided to leave, commit to going out of contact with the narcissist. Cut off all forms of communication, including phone calls, text messages, emails, and social media interactions. Avoid seeking closure or explanations from the narcissist, as this can prolong your emotional distress and make it harder to move

on. Instead, focus on protecting yourself and creating a clean break from the toxic relationship.

10. **Don't let them back in.** Despite your best efforts to go no-contact, the narcissist may attempt to hoover you back into the relationship through love bombing, manipulation, or promises of change. Stay firm in your decision to leave and resist the temptation to reengage with the narcissist. Remember that their behavior is likely to remain unchanged, and allowing them back into your life will only perpetuate the cycle of abuse.

11. **Get ready for retaliation.** Leaving a narcissist can trigger feelings of anger, resentment, and revenge in the narcissist. Be prepared for potential retaliation tactics, such as smear campaigns, harassment, or legal threats. Take steps to protect yourself by documenting any incidents of retaliation and seeking legal advice if necessary. Surround yourself with a supportive network of friends, family, and professionals who can offer guidance and assistance during this challenging time.

12. **Put away reminders of the relationship.** Remove any reminders of the relationship from your living space, including gifts, photographs, and sentimental items. Clearing out these physical reminders can help create a sense of closure and facilitate the healing process. Consider engaging in activities that bring you joy and fulfillment, such as pursuing hobbies, spending time with loved ones, or practicing self-care rituals.

13. **Choose your battles carefully when co-parenting.** If you share children with the narcissist, navigating

co-parenting can present additional challenges. While it's important to prioritize your children's well-being, be selective about engaging with the narcissist and set clear boundaries to protect yourself from further abuse.

HOW TO LEAVE EVEN IF YOU STILL LOVE THE NARCISSIST

Michaela, one of the women in my community help group, shared with us how to leave a narcissist even if you still love them. She said:

> I can speak to this because two years after leaving my narcissistic partner, I still tend to miss him sometimes, but I know the abuse he subjected me to cannot make me want to go back. Now, if I randomly think of him two years later, you can imagine how hard it was to leave then.

Michaela's story began with her recognizing the pattern of abuse in her relationship:

> At first, I didn't want to see it. I was so deeply in love with him, and he had a way of making me feel like I was the only one who truly mattered to him. But then, the criticism started—the belittling, the constant need to put me down to feel superior. It was soul-crushing, yet I kept holding on to the good moments, hoping they would return.

When Michaela decided it was time to leave, she knew it wouldn't be easy:

I had to come to terms with the fact that love alone wasn't enough to sustain a healthy relationship. Loving him didn't mean I had to endure the abuse. It was a hard pill to swallow, but I had to remind myself daily that I deserved better.

The first thing I had to do was acknowledge the reality of the abuse. I made a list of all the instances where he had hurt me, both emotionally and physically. Seeing it all written down helped me realize that the relationship was toxic and harmful, no matter how much I loved him.

I reached out to my close friends and family for support. I told them what I was going through and asked for their help. Their love and encouragement gave me the strength to take the next steps. I also joined a support group, which was incredibly validating and empowering.

Leaving a narcissist requires careful planning. I started saving money discreetly and looked for a safe place to stay. I made sure to gather all the important documents and valuables I might need after leaving. This preparation was crucial in ensuring that I could leave without looking back.

I knew that telling him I was leaving could provoke a dangerous reaction, so I decided not to inform him in advance. Once I left, I blocked his number and all forms of communication. It was painful but necessary. I needed a clean break to start healing.

Therapy played a big role in my recovery. My therapist helped me understand the dynamics of narcissistic abuse and how to rebuild my self-esteem. She also taught me coping strategies to deal with the emotional aftermath of leaving someone I still had feelings for.

I had to relearn how to take care of myself. I started doing things I loved—things that made me happy and fulfilled. I took up new hobbies, reconnected with old friends, and prioritized my mental and physical well-being.

There were days when I missed him terribly, but I kept reminding myself why I left. I read the list of abusive incidents and reminded myself that no amount of love could justify staying in such a toxic relationship. I deserved respect, love, and kindness, and I wouldn't settle for less.

Leaving someone you love, especially a narcissist, is incredibly challenging. But it's possible. It's about choosing yourself, your happiness, and your well-being over the toxic love you once had. It's a journey, but each step away from the abuse is a step toward a better, healthier life.

HOW TO NEVER GO BACK TO A NARCISSIST

The fact that you were attracted to that person, built so many memories together, and perhaps have a family with them may give you ideas to go back to them. Sometimes, the narcissist may persuade you and tell you how they have changed, luring you back in. It has happened to a great number of people. Many have walked back into toxic relationships, but it should not be the case with you. Here is how to never go back to a narcissist.

The first step to ensuring you never return to a narcissist is to remember why you left in the first place. Keep a journal or a list of all the abusive behaviors, manipulations, and betrayals you endured. Reflect on how these experiences affected your mental and physical health. Whenever you feel the urge to go back, read through these notes to remind yourself of the pain and suffering you escaped from.

Surround yourself with friends, family, and support groups who understand your situation and can provide emotional support. These people can offer perspective, advice, and encouragement when you feel vulnerable or uncertain about your decision. Lean on them during tough times, and don't hesitate to ask for help when you need it.

Establish clear boundaries with your narcissistic ex and stick to them. This might mean going no-contact or limiting communication to only necessary interactions, especially if children are involved. Blocking their number, unfollowing them on social media, and avoiding places where you might run into them can help you maintain these boundaries.

Dedicate time and effort to your personal growth and healing. Engage in activities that bring you joy and fulfillment. Pursue hobbies, interests, and goals you may have neglected during the toxic relationship. This will boost your self-esteem and help you rediscover your identity and independence.

Visualize and plan for the future without your narcissistic ex. Set new goals and dreams that do not include them. Focus on building a life that aligns with your values and desires. This future-oriented mindset can keep you motivated to stay away from the past and move toward a healthier, happier life.

Forgive yourself for any mistakes or perceived shortcomings in the relationship. Understand that falling for a narcissist does not mean you are weak or foolish. It means you are human. Self-forgiveness is a crucial step in healing and moving forward.

Continue educating yourself about narcissistic abuse and recovery. The more you know, the better equipped you are to recognize red flags and protect yourself from future toxic relationships.

As we transition from learning how to escape a narcissist's trap, it's crucial to understand what comes next. Leaving a narcissistic relationship is a significant and brave step, but it is only the beginning of your healing journey. Each time I hear stories of survivors, the common thread is the realization that the battle is far from over once they walk away. This brings us to the next important phase: acknowledging the aftermath.

CHAPTER 4

A—ACKNOWLEDGE THE AFTERMATH

"View your life as a toxic-free zone! If someone treats you badly, don't lower yourself to their level. Stay toxicity-free. Simply do what you can to move on."

KAREN SALMANSOHN

Moving away is not the end of the battle with narcissism—the real fight is in healing. Michaela's journey illustrates this truth all too well. Here is Michaela detailing her struggle in the aftermath of leaving her narcissistic partner:

Leaving Joe was the hardest decision I've ever made, but I knew I had to do it for my own sanity. I thought once I walked out the door, the worst would be over. I couldn't have been more wrong. The real struggle began the moment I stepped into my new apartment, alone and vulnerable.

The first few weeks were a blur of emotions. I felt a

strange mix of relief and emptiness. My self-esteem, already battered by years of Joe's manipulation and emotional abuse, was at an all-time low. I couldn't look in the mirror without hearing his cruel words echoing in my mind. He had convinced me that I was worthless, and it took every ounce of my strength to remind myself that I deserved better.

I struggled with trust issues, not just with others but also with myself. I doubted every decision I made, fearing that I would somehow end up in another toxic relationship. The trauma from Joe's constant gaslighting left me questioning my own reality. Simple tasks like going grocery shopping or talking to a neighbor felt overwhelming.

Nights were the worst. Alone with my thoughts, I replayed every argument and degrading comment, wondering what I could have done differently. Sleep was a distant memory, replaced by anxiety and nightmares. The isolation was suffocating, and I often found myself missing Joe despite everything. I missed the person he pretended to be, the person I fell in love with.

When I tried to talk to friends and family, I felt misunderstood. They were supportive, but they couldn't grasp the depth of my pain or the complexity of my feelings. How could I explain that I still loved the man who had caused me so much harm? It felt like a betrayal of myself to even think of it.

I joined a support group, hoping to find solace among others who had been through similar experiences. It helped to some extent, but I still felt like I was walking through a fog, struggling to find clarity and direction.

> The real fight was in learning to heal, to rebuild my
> sense of self-worth, and to believe I was more than
> Joe's cruel assessment of me.

Michaela's story highlights the immense challenges she faced after leaving a narcissistic relationship. This chapter aims to guide you through the aftermath, helping you understand that the battle doesn't end with leaving the abuser. Healing is a complex journey that requires time, patience, and effort.

THE AFTERMATH OF LEAVING AN ABUSIVE RELATIONSHIP

Once you leave an abusive relationship, you might find yourself on an emotional rollercoaster. Feelings of relief and liberation can quickly be overshadowed by confusion, guilt, and even longing for the abuser. It's common to question your decision, wondering if things could have been different. This emotional upheaval is a normal part of the healing process. Remember, your mind and heart are working through years of manipulation and trauma.

Abusers often erode your self-esteem, leaving you feeling unworthy and powerless. After leaving, these feelings don't just disappear. You might struggle with self-doubt, question your decision-making abilities, and mistrust your judgment. The negative self-image painted by your abuser can linger, making it hard to see yourself as the strong, capable person you truly are.

Trusting others, and even yourself, can become a significant hurdle. The constant gaslighting and manipulation you endured might make you wary of people's intentions, fearing you'll end up in another toxic relationship. This lack of trust can extend to friends and family, creating a sense of isolation even when loved ones surround you.

Despite the abuse, it's normal to grieve the end of the relationship. You might miss the moments of affection or the hope that things would get better. This grieving process can be confusing as you reconcile feelings of love and attachment with the reality of the abuse you suffered. Understanding it's okay to grieve can be vital in your healing journey.

Starting over can be terrifying. The fear of the unknown, combined with the comfort of familiarity, might tempt you to return to the abuser. It's essential to remind yourself of why you left and focus on the possibilities that lie ahead. Embrace this new chapter as an opportunity to rediscover yourself and build a life free from abuse.

Apart from emotional struggles, practical challenges can also arise. You might face financial instability, housing issues, or custody battles if children are involved. These practicalities can add stress, but seeking help from legal and social services can provide the support you need to navigate these difficulties.

LONG-TERM EFFECTS AND CHALLENGES TO HEALING

Healing is an individual journey. We all heal on our own timelines. For some, it may come relatively easily, while for others, it can take much longer. Along this path, various challenges arise that make the healing journey harder than it already is. These challenges, coupled with the long-term effects of narcissistic abuse, can make recovery seem like an uphill battle.

Jeff: Anxiety and Depression

It's been almost a year since I left my narcissistic partner, but the effects of that toxic relationship still haunt me. I often wake up in the middle of the night, heart racing, drenched in sweat, as if I'm still trapped in that never-ending cycle of manipulation and abuse. My anxiety can be crippling. I find myself constantly on edge, waiting for the next shoe to drop, even though I'm no longer with them. Simple tasks, like going to the grocery store or answering the phone, can trigger waves of panic.

The depression is another beast entirely. Some days, it feels like a heavy fog has settled over my mind, making it hard to see any joy or purpose in life. Getting out of bed takes a monumental effort, and I struggle to find motivation for things I used to love. My friends don't always understand why I'm still so affected, but it's like the scars are etched deep into my soul.

Lena: Lingering Trauma

Even though I managed to escape my narcissistic husband three years ago, the trauma lingers. Sometimes, when I hear a specific tone of voice or see certain mannerisms, I'm immediately transported back to those terrifying moments. I get flashbacks that make me feel like I'm right back in that house, walking on eggshells, trying to avoid setting him off. Nightmares are a common occurrence, and I often wake up feeling as exhausted as when I went to sleep.

My therapist says these are normal responses to prolonged trauma, but that doesn't make them any easier to deal with. The hypervigilance, the jumpiness—it all feels like my mind is stuck in survival mode, even though I'm safe now. I've found some solace in trauma-focused therapy, and slowly, I'm learning to trust the present and let go of the past.

Mark: Attachment Issues

Forming new relationships after leaving my narcissistic ex-wife has been incredibly challenging. The constant need for validation and the fear of being hurt again has made me extremely cautious. I find it hard to let people in, always expecting them to betray or abandon me, just like she did. This fear often leads to isolation, even when I desperately crave connection. I've realized that I need to rebuild my ability to trust, both in others and in myself. It's not an easy road.

Mia: Self-Esteem and Identity Crisis

After years of being belittled and controlled by my narcissistic partner, my self-esteem was shattered. I used to be confident and outgoing, but now I constantly doubt my worth and abilities. It's like I lost a part of myself in that relationship, and I'm struggling to find it again. Every mistake feels like a confirmation of my inadequacy, and every compliment feels undeserved. I've started journaling and practicing affirmations to remind myself of my strengths, but it's a slow process.

Rebuilding a positive self-image after such intense emotional abuse is like piecing together a broken mirror—each shard is a painful reminder of what was. However, each day, I see a little more of the person I used to be before the abuse took its toll.

Sarah: Fear of Repeating Patterns

One of my biggest fears after leaving my narcissistic partner is falling into the same type of relationship again. I'm hyper-aware of the patterns of manipulation and control now, but that awareness comes with its own set of anxieties. I second-guess every new person I meet, constantly searching for red flags and questioning my judgment.

This fear of repeating past mistakes makes it hard to trust anyone, including myself. I've become overly cautious, sometimes to the point of pushing people away who might actually be good for me. To combat this, I've been working on recognizing and setting healthy boundaries and taking things slow in any new relationship.

Jasmine: Financial and Practical Challenges

Leaving my narcissistic husband meant starting from scratch financially. He had control over all our finances, so I had nothing but the clothes on my back when I left. Rebuilding my life has been incredibly tough. Finding a job, securing a place to live, and reestablishing my credit have all been uphill battles.

Sometimes, I doubted whether I made the right decision because of these practical challenges.

I've had to seek assistance from financial advisors and community resources to get back on my feet. It's been humbling but empowering to take control of my financial future. Each small victory, like getting my own bank account or securing a stable job, has been a step toward reclaiming my independence.

Alex: Difficulty Setting Boundaries

Setting boundaries has been one of my biggest challenges since leaving my narcissistic partner. Years of being conditioned to put their needs above my own made it hard for me to even recognize my boundaries, let alone enforce them. I often felt guilty for asserting myself and feared repercussions for doing so.

I've started practicing by setting small boundaries in safe environments, like with close friends or at work. This has helped build my confidence and made establishing and maintaining healthy boundaries in all areas of my life easier. It's still a work in progress, but I'm learning that my needs and limits are valid and deserve respect.

KEY ACTIVITIES THAT WILL HELP YOU HEAL

Healing from narcissistic abuse requires effort, and I have to be honest with you: You must be willing to go the extra mile to heal. It's not all about leaving your narcissistic partner and thinking that you are suddenly free. From the scenarios above, we observe that the lingering effects can stick for a long time. This means we should take the onus upon ourselves to heal. In my experiences and interactions with victims of abuse, I have learned that these are the primary areas of focus when healing: practicing self-love and self-care, reclaiming your identity and independence, and rebuilding self-esteem.

Practicing Self-Love and Self-Care

One of the most crucial aspects of healing is learning to love and care for yourself. Narcissistic abuse often leaves victims feeling unworthy and unlovable. Rebuilding a loving relationship with yourself is the first step toward recovery.

Caitlyn realized that she had been her harshest critic. The constant belittlement and criticism from her narcissistic partner had made her internalize negative thoughts about herself. To counteract this, she began practicing self-compassion. Here is how she reinforced self-love and care:

Every morning, I stood in front of my mirror and repeated positive affirmations. Phrases like "I am worthy," "I am enough," and "I deserve happiness" became my daily mantras. This practice helped me rewire my brain to think positively about myself.
I learned to acknowledge my emotions without judgment. On days when I felt overwhelmed by sadness or anger, I allowed myself to cry or vent without feeling guilty. I understood that my feelings were valid and essential to my healing process.
I made sure to get enough rest and sleep. I realized that my body needed time to recover from the years of stress and anxiety. I established a bedtime routine

that included turning off electronic devices an hour before bed and practicing deep-breathing exercises to help me sleep better.

Rediscovering my passions was a significant step in my healing journey. I signed up for painting classes, something I had always wanted to do but never had the time or confidence for. Immersing myself in creativity helped me express my emotions and provided a sense of accomplishment.

I started taking regular walks in nature. Being outdoors, surrounded by the beauty of the natural world, was incredibly soothing. It gave me a sense of peace and allowed me to reconnect with myself. Creating a daily routine was crucial for me to regain a sense of normalcy and control. I set a structured daily schedule that balanced work, self-care, and leisure activities. A routine helped me stay grounded and gave me a sense of purpose each day. Additionally, I incorporated journaling into my routine. Writing down my thoughts and feelings allowed me to process my emotions and track my progress. Reflecting on my journey and celebrating my small victories became a therapeutic outlet.

Reclaiming Your Identity and Independence

The healing journey calls you to reimmerse yourself into the person you should be. You deserve to free yourself from the expectations of your narcissist and run your life in a way that you choose to. Here is how Caitlyn managed to navigate her way around this:

Reclaiming my identity and independence was a pivotal part of my healing journey. For so long, I had lost sight of who I was and what I wanted out of life. But breaking free from the narcissistic relationship allowed me to rediscover myself and reclaim my autonomy.

I focused on setting boundaries and asserting my needs in all areas of my life. This meant learning to say no without guilt, advocating for myself in relationships and at work, and prioritizing my well-being above all else. Taking control of my life and making decisions aligned with my values and desires was empowering. Furthermore, I consciously tried to surround myself with supportive and nurturing relationships. I sought out friends and family who uplifted me, validated my experiences, and encouraged my growth. Building a strong support system was essential in helping me navigate the challenges of healing and rebuilding my life after abuse.

Finally, I embraced the journey of self-discovery and personal growth. I committed myself to lifelong learning and self-improvement, whether through therapy, self-help books, or workshops and seminars. By investing in my development, I gained a deeper understanding of myself and cultivated the confidence and resilience needed to thrive independently.

Rebuilding Your Self-Esteem

Once you have taken control of your identity and guaranteed your independence, the perfect direction is toward rebuilding your self-esteem. You need to re-establish that confidence in yourself and your overall goals. Here is how Caitlyn did so:

> After years of being undermined and invalidated by my narcissistic partner, I had internalized a deep sense of worthlessness and self-doubt. But through dedication and self-reflection, I gradually rebuilt my confidence and rediscovered my inherent value.
> One of my first steps was to challenge the negative beliefs and inner critic that had taken root in my mind. I practiced self-compassion and self-acceptance, reminding myself that I deserved love and respect just as I was. Instead of dwelling on my perceived flaws and shortcomings, I focused on my strengths and unique qualities, celebrating my progress and accomplishments along the way.
> I also surrounded myself with positivity and affirmation, seeking out sources of encouragement and validation in my daily life. Whether through affirmations, supportive friendships, or empowering literature, I consciously tried to cultivate a nurturing environment that uplifted and empowered me.
> Moreover, I challenged myself to step outside my comfort zone and pursue growth opportunities that stretched my capabilities and expanded my horizons. Whether taking on new challenges at work, volunteering in my community, or pursuing personal goals, I proved to myself that I was capable, competent, and deserving of success.

SHOULD YOU FORGIVE THE NARCISSIST?

Forgiving a narcissistic partner can be a complex and deeply personal decision, one that often evokes conflicting emotions and uncertainties. Ultimately, forgiveness is not about condoning or excusing the narcissist's harmful behavior; rather, it's about releasing yourself from the grip of resentment, anger, and pain that can keep you trapped in the past.

When you forgive, you're not letting the narcissist off the hook or minimizing the impact of their actions. Instead, you're prioritizing your healing and well-being by relinquishing the negative emotions that bind you to the past. Forgiveness is a gift you give yourself—a way to reclaim your power and control over your life.

By forgiving the narcissist, you're freeing yourself from the burden of carrying around resentment and bitterness. You're choosing to let go of the emotional baggage that weighs you down and prevents you from fully moving forward. Forgiveness allows you to release the hold that the narcissist and the past have over you, enabling you to embrace the present moment and create a brighter future for yourself.

Forgiveness doesn't mean you have to reconcile with the narcissist or maintain any contact with them. It's entirely possible to forgive someone from a distance without ever engaging with them again. Forgiveness is a personal journey you undertake for your own sake, regardless of the narcissist's actions or intentions.

That being said, forgiveness is not always easy, and it may take time to fully let go of the pain and hurt inflicted by the narcissist. It's okay to acknowledge your feelings and grieve the loss of the relationship and the dreams you once had.

In the next chapter, we focus on the importance of prioritizing your mental health after leaving a narcissistic relationship. Learn how to nurture your well-being, build resilience, and cultivate inner strength as you embark on your journey of healing and self-discovery.

BREAKOUT BREAK

"We can all fight against loneliness by engaging in random acts of kindness."

GAIL HONEYMAN

Being in a relationship with someone who's constantly manipulating you and making you question everything about yourself is, as I'm sure you know, incredibly isolating. For many people that isolation is literal: Their partner has done everything they can to cut them off from friends and family, and they feel totally dependent on them for love and support. I hope you're not in this situation yourself, but I know there's a high chance you may be... and if you're not, I've no doubt there have been times you've felt isolated regardless. How can you talk about what's been happening to you when half the time you're not even sure if it's really happening or if it's all in your own mind? Even if you did, you'd feel guilty for showing your partner in this light. Instead, you find yourself defending them, telling a story that even you start to believe.

This kind of relationship dynamic affects far more people than it should, and the saddest thing is that many people suffering from narcissistic abuse aren't even sure they're experiencing it. I want to offer a lifeline to all of those people. I want to show them that their experience is real and valid, and I want to help them find a way out. Having been in this situation yourself, you're the best person to help me do this, and I know that once you're through the other side of this, you'll be keen on spotting the warning signs in other people. You may not be there quite yet, but there's still a way you can help now.

By leaving a review of this book on Amazon, you'll show other people where they can find this lifeline, and you'll help them answer any questions they still have about whether they too are experiencing narcissistic abuse.

Reviews help connect readers with the information they're looking for, so your words could make more of a difference than you realize. This is a very isolating situation for anyone to be in, and your words will let them know they're not alone, at the same time as showing them exactly where they can find the guidance they need.

Thank you so much for your support. If we work together, we can all move forward to a brighter future.

Scan the QR code below

CHAPTER 5

K—KEEP YOURSELF HOLISTICALLY HEALTHY

"It's not about how fast you're moving. As long as you're moving toward your goals, you're making yourself better. That's all that matters. Being healthy and strong is a lifelong journey, so you don't have to rush."

ANONYMOUS

Each time I think about the mental toll narcissistic abuse takes, I remember Hillary's story. Here it is in her own words.

I used to be the life of the party, full of laughter and energy. But after years of being in a relationship with a narcissistic partner, my spark dimmed. I started doubting myself, feeling worthless, and being constantly anxious. It wasn't until I decided to prioritize my mental health that things began to change. I realized that I had been subjected to various narcissistic abuse tactics, such as gaslighting and emotional manipulation, which severely deteriorated my self-image and mental well-being. I took the brave step of seeking professional help and engaging in self-care activities. By nurturing my self-esteem and setting healthy boundaries, I began to reclaim my life. I found solace in activities I loved, reconnected with supportive friends, and practiced mindfulness to stay grounded.

The transformation was incredible. My confidence returned, and I became more resilient. While narcissistic abuse left deep scars, prioritizing my mental health and self-care led to profound healing and growth.

This chapter is designed to guide you through understanding the mental health impact of narcissistic abuse and to provide you with practical steps for nurturing your well-being.

SELF-CARE AFTER NARCISSISTIC ABUSE TRAUMA

Healing from narcissistic abuse is no walk in the park. It's messy, painful, and absolutely essential. If you think you can just walk away from a narcissist and immediately be okay, think again. The scars they leave aren't just skin deep; they burrow into your psyche, sense of self, and ability to trust the world around you. That's why self-care isn't just important—it's non-negotiable. You need to be willing to fight for your mental health and well-being with everything you've got.

Self-care after narcissistic abuse trauma isn't about spa days and bubble baths, although those can be nice. It's about reclaiming your life, rebuilding your sense of self, and nurturing the parts of you that have been battered and bruised. It's hard work and requires tough love, discipline, and a fierce commitment to putting yourself first.

Self-care is a multifaceted approach to healing that encompasses various aspects of your life. It's not limited to taking care of your physical body; it calls for nurturing every part of yourself to achieve overall well-being and become the best version of yourself. By incorporating physical, spiritual, social, emotional, and mental self-care into your routine, you create a holistic approach to healing. Each aspect of self-care is interconnected, and together, they contribute to your overall well-being. This balanced approach helps you rebuild your sense of self, boosts your resilience, and fosters a healthier, happier life.

Physical self-care involves activities that improve your physical health. These include exercise, proper nutrition, adequate sleep, and regular medical check-ups. When you take care of your body, you feel more energetic, resilient, and capable of handling stress. It's about honoring your body's needs and treating it with the respect it deserves.

Spiritual self-care is finding a sense of purpose and connection beyond yourself. This can involve practices like meditation, prayer, spending time in nature, or exploring spiritual or religious beliefs. Engaging in spiritual self-care can bring peace, clarity, and a deeper understanding of yourself and the world around you.

Humans are inherently social creatures, and building meaningful connections is vital for our well-being. Social self-care involves nurturing supportive, positive, and enriching relationships. This can mean spending time with friends and family, joining a club or group, or simply reaching out to loved ones. Healthy social interactions can boost your mood and provide a network of support.

Emotional self-care focuses on understanding and managing your emotions. It involves activities that help you process and express your feelings in healthy ways. This can include journaling, talking to a therapist, practicing mindfulness, or engaging in hobbies that bring you joy. By prioritizing your emotional health, you can navigate life's challenges with greater ease and resilience.

Mental self-care is about keeping your mind sharp and healthy. This can be achieved through activities that stimulate your intellect and creativity, such as reading, learning new skills, solving puzzles, or engaging in creative arts. It's also about managing stress and avoiding mental exhaustion by setting boundaries and taking breaks when needed.

All aspects of health are connected, forming a comprehensive framework for overall well-being. When you prioritize physical health, you find the energy and resilience to tackle emotional and mental challenges. Engaging in spiritual practices can bring clarity and peace, helping you process and heal from trauma. Social connections provide essential support and validation, reinforcing your sense of belonging and self-worth.

I challenge you to write down one goal for each category—physical, spiritual, social, emotional, and mental—that you can start implementing today. These small goals will lead to little victories, boosting your self-confidence and fostering a sense of independence.

For instance, your physical goal might be to take a daily walk, while your spiritual goal could involve five minutes of meditation each morning. Socially, you might aim to reach out to a friend or join a new group. Emotionally, consider starting a journal, and mentally, commit to reading a book or learning a new skill.

These small steps pave the way for profound changes, enhance your holistic health, and empower you on your healing journey.

BUILD YOUR SUPPORT NETWORK

More than ever before in your life, you need a strong support system when overcoming narcissistic abuse. It's easier to break down or fall back into the narcissist's traps if you don't have a dependable support network. However, keep in mind that this is not a cue for codependency—you've fought hard to break free from that cycle, and you don't want to fall back into old patterns.

A strong support network provides emotional backing, practical advice, and a sense of belonging, all crucial for your healing journey. Here's why having this network is vital:

- **Emotional Support:** Friends and family who understand your situation can offer empathy and validation, helping you process your emotions and experiences.
- **Practical Assistance:** Supportive individuals can provide practical help, whether assisting with daily tasks, offering a safe space, or helping you navigate legal or financial matters.

- **Accountability:** A strong network keeps you accountable in your healing process, reminding you of your progress and encouraging you to maintain boundaries.
- **Encouragement and Motivation:** Supportive people can inspire you to stay committed to your self-care routines and personal growth goals.

When Caitlyn left her narcissistic partner, she realized the importance of surrounding herself with positive, supportive people. She reached out to close friends who had always been there for her but whom she had distanced herself from during her abusive relationship. Reconnecting with these friends provided her with a safe space to share her experiences and receive much-needed empathy and encouragement.

Caitlyn also joined an online support group for survivors of narcissistic abuse. In this group, she found a community of individuals who understood her struggles and offered practical advice and emotional support. This network became crucial to her healing journey, helping her feel less isolated and more empowered.

She also sought professional help from a therapist who specialized in trauma and narcissistic abuse recovery. Through regular sessions, she learned coping mechanisms and strategies to rebuild her self-esteem and trust in herself.

Here are some steps to build and maintain a healthy support network without falling into codependency:

- Start by identifying the people in your life who genuinely care about your well-being. These could be friends, family members, colleagues, or even neighbors who have shown consistent kindness and support.
- Consider joining support groups, either in person or online, where you can connect with others who have experienced similar situations. These groups provide a safe space to share your story, receive advice, and learn from others' experiences.
- Therapists, counselors, and coaches who specialize in narcissistic abuse recovery can provide professional guidance and support. They can help you develop coping strategies, work through trauma, and rebuild your self-esteem.
- Ensure that your relationships are based on mutual respect and support. Set clear boundaries to protect your emotional well-being, and communicate your needs and limits to avoid falling back into codependent behaviors.
- Maintain regular contact with your support network. Regular check-ins, whether through phone calls, messages, or meet-ups, can strengthen your connections and provide continuous support.
- Being open about your feelings and experiences helps your support network understand what you're going through and how they can best support you. Honesty fosters trust and deeper connections.

NURTURE YOUR SELF-ESTEEM

As we have already seen, narcissistic abuse will wear down your self-esteem, causing you to lose your confidence and that inner glow that once defined you. Rebuilding your self-esteem is essential for reclaiming your life and sense of self-worth.

Self-esteem impacts every aspect of life, from personal relationships to professional achievements. Here, Milly shares her story and how she nurtured her self-esteem:

I want to share my journey of reclaiming my self-esteem after years of narcissistic abuse from my ex-husband. It was a tough road, but by focusing on certain key areas, I rebuilt my confidence and self-worth. Here's how I did it.

One of the first things I had to do was recognize the situations that negatively impacted my self-esteem. Living with a narcissistic partner meant I was constantly belittled and criticized, which took a huge toll on my sense of self-worth.

I noticed that my self-esteem plummeted whenever I was in social settings where my ex would undermine me in front of friends or family. Recognizing these situations helped me understand the environments and interactions that harmed my self-esteem.

After recognizing these situations, I had to become aware of the thoughts and beliefs they triggered. I realized that my ex's constant criticism had planted deep-seated negative beliefs about myself in my mind. I would often think, "I'm not good enough," or "I can't do anything right." These thoughts had become automatic responses to any challenge or setback I faced. Challenging these negative thoughts was crucial. I had to learn to question their validity and replace them with more positive and realistic beliefs.

Whenever I caught myself thinking, "I'm not good enough," I would challenge that thought by listing things I had accomplished or was good at. I would remind myself of times when I had succeeded and been praised by others.

Over time, I started to adjust my thoughts and beliefs. This wasn't an overnight change; it took consistent effort and practice.

I started practicing mindfulness meditation. Each day, I dedicated a few minutes to sit quietly and focus on my breathing, letting go of any negative thoughts that surfaced. This practice helped me become more aware of my emotions and less reactive to the triggers that used to undermine my self-worth. Gradually, mindfulness meditation began to replace the negative self-talk that had dominated my mind for so long, helping to rebuild my self-esteem.

Rebuilding my self-esteem after narcissistic abuse was one of the hardest things I've ever done, but it was also the most rewarding. By recognizing the situations that affected my self-esteem, becoming aware of my thoughts and beliefs, challenging negative thinking, and adjusting my thoughts and beliefs, I was able to reclaim my confidence and sense of self-worth.

If you're on a similar journey, I encourage you to be patient with yourself. Healing takes time, but every step you take toward nurturing your self-esteem is a step toward a stronger, more empowered you.

FACE YOUR INSECURITIES

Insecurities are feelings of uncertainty or anxiety about oneself; they often stem from doubts about our abilities, worth, or appearance. These feelings can undermine our confidence and prevent us from fully engaging in life.

Narcissistic abuse can severely damage our self-esteem, leading to deep-seated insecurities. A narcissist's constant criticism, belittling, and manipulation create an environment where we start doubting our value and capabilities. Over time, these negative experiences can erode our confidence, leaving us feeling insecure and unworthy.

Running away from our insecurities only prolongs the healing process. Ignoring or avoiding them allows these negative feelings to fester and grow, making it even harder to overcome them. Facing our insecurities head-on is crucial for healing and rebuilding our self-worth.

You no longer need to feel trapped by the shadows of your past. The chains of narcissistic abuse can be broken, and you hold the key. It's time to embrace your power and make the changes necessary to start healing and reclaiming your life.

Milly had been incredibly hard on herself for years. The constant belittlement and criticism from her narcissistic ex-husband made her internalize negative thoughts about herself. To counteract this, she began practicing self-compassion. Milly realized that insecurities often feel like insurmountable obstacles, but what if she viewed them differently? She decided to think of them as markers on her journey to self-discovery and strength. Each time she faced an insecurity, she saw it as a chance to learn more about herself and grow stronger. This mindset shift transformed her insecurities from sources of fear into challenges to conquer.

Surviving narcissistic abuse was a testament to Milly's strength and resilience. She reminded herself that she'd already faced some of the toughest challenges, which meant she had the inner strength to confront her insecurities. Each morning, she stood in front of her mirror and repeated positive affirmations. Phrases like "I am worthy," "I am enough," and "I deserve happiness" became her daily mantras. This practice helped rewire her brain to think positively about herself.

Every small step Milly took toward facing insecurity became a victory. On days when she spoke up in meetings or set boundaries with friends, she celebrated her courage. These small successes built her confidence and showed her she could overcome her insecurities.

Milly learned to replace self-criticism with self-compassion. She treated herself with the same kindness and understanding she would offer a friend. She acknowledged that everyone has insecurities and that facing them is brave. Whenever she felt overwhelmed by sadness or anger, she allowed herself to cry or vent without feeling guilty. She understood that her feelings were valid and essential to her healing process.

Building a support network was crucial for Milly. She surrounded herself with friends who uplifted and encouraged her. Their positive reinforcement bolstered her confidence and gave her the strength to face her insecurities. She knew that she was not alone on this journey.

Setting small, achievable goals helped Milly address her insecurities step by step. For example, if she felt insecure about speaking in public, she started by expressing her thoughts in small group settings. Gradually, she increased the scale of her challenges as her confidence grew. Achieving these goals reinforced her belief in her abilities.

Milly embraced vulnerability, understanding that it was not a sign of weakness but a sign of strength. When she allowed herself to be vulnerable, she opened up to genuine connections and experiences. She embraced vulnerability as a necessary step toward growth and healing.

The process of facing insecurities was a learning journey for Milly. Some strategies worked better than others, and that was okay. She was willing to adapt and find what worked best for her. This flexibility helped her develop resilience and problem-solving skills.

The healing journey continues with Chapter 6. This chapter focuses on the empowering process of taking control of your story and rebuilding your identity after narcissistic abuse. It's about reclaiming the power taken from you and writing a new chapter in your life, one where you are the protagonist, not the victim.

CHAPTER 6
0—OWN YOUR NARRATIVE: RECLAIMING SELF AFTER ABUSE

"I like stories where women save themselves."

NEIL GAIMAN

Murphy, a friend I made while writing this book, embodies the journey of losing and then fighting to regain one's power and identity.

Murphy was a vibrant, confident man when he met Lisa. Her charm and apparent confidence drew him in. At first, everything seemed perfect. However, as time went on, Lisa's true nature began to surface. She was a classic narcissist, using manipulation, gaslighting, and emotional abuse to control Murphy. Slowly but surely, Murphy started to lose himself.

Lisa's constant narcissism made Murphy doubt his abilities and worth. She would undermine his accomplishments and make him feel like he couldn't do anything right without her. Over time, Murphy's self-esteem plummeted. He stopped engaging in activities he once loved, avoided friends and family, and began to feel like a shadow of his former self.

The worst part was that Murphy didn't realize how much he had changed. He was so entrenched in the toxic relationship that he couldn't see how much of his power and identity he had surrendered. It wasn't until one night, after yet another argument where Lisa had made him feel worthless, that Murphy had an epiphany. He looked in the mirror and didn't recognize the person staring back at him. It was at that moment he realized he had to reclaim his life.

Reclaiming your power means writing a new narrative for yourself. Murphy decided to see his past not as a series of defeats but as a testament to his resilience and strength. He embraced his journey, learned from it, and used it to fuel his growth.

This chapter is about empowering you to do the same. You have the strength within you to reclaim your narrative and write your story on your terms.

RECONNECT AND EMBRACE YOUR OWN IDENTITY AFTER THE ABUSE

It's no secret that narcissistic abuse can make us unrecognizable, causing us to lose our own identity. It transforms us into someone we never thought we could be, chipping away at our self-esteem and sense of self. To overcome the aftermath of this abuse, you must reconnect with and embrace your own identity. Instead of becoming who you used to be, understand that your experiences have changed you and that you can decide whether you change for the better or the worse. We can't go back and make different choices or change what we've been through, but we can choose to learn and grow from even the worst experiences. The goal should be to come out even stronger than before, not despite what happened but because it happened.

From my own experiences and observing those around me, I've observed that there are four crucial steps when reconnecting with yourself following an escape from narcissistic abuse. These steps serve as guiding principles on the journey to reclaiming your identity and rebuilding your life:

Step 1: Reflect on Who You Were

Reflecting on who you were before the abuse is a crucial first step in reclaiming your identity. Take a moment to dip into your memories and recall the person you once were—the passions, dreams, and aspirations that defined you. For Murphy, this meant revisiting his dream of becoming a teacher and his passion for helping others learn and grow. Before the abuse, Murphy was energetic and proactive, always seeking opportunities to positively impact others' lives. During the abusive relationship, these characteristics were overshadowed, and he found himself losing touch with his core values and aspirations. As Murphy reminisced about his goal of making a difference in the world through teaching, he started reconnecting with his true self's essence. This reflection marked the beginning of his journey to reclaim his identity and rediscover his inner strength.

Step 2: Revisit Old Hobbies and Interests

Rediscovering the activities that once brought you joy is another vital step in reconnecting with yourself. Whether painting, writing, gardening, or any other hobby, immersing yourself in these pastimes can reignite your passion and revive your sense of self. For Murphy, this meant revisiting his love for playing the guitar and the solace he found in music. These activities provided a space for him to reconnect with his inner self, free from the constraints of the abusive past.

Step 3: Set New Goals

Embracing a future filled with possibilities begins with setting new goals. These goals can be personal, professional, or a combination of both. They provide a roadmap for your journey forward and empower you to take control of your life once again. For Murphy, setting the goal of learning a new piece on the guitar and hiking a new trail each month became a source of motivation and inspiration. These goals gave him a sense of purpose and served as tangible reminders of his resilience and determination to thrive despite past challenges. By setting new goals, you, too, can pave the way for a brighter, more fulfilling future.

Step 4: Embrace Your Strength and Resilience

Acknowledge and celebrate the strength and resilience that have carried you through your journey. Every obstacle you've overcome and every setback you've faced has contributed to the person you are today. Embrace the lessons from your experiences and allow them to fuel your growth and transformation. By acknowledging your inner strength and resilience, you empower yourself to navigate future challenges with courage and confidence. Remember, you are stronger than you think, and you have the power to overcome anything life throws your way.

RECLAIM YOUR POWER AFTER THE TRAUMA

Reclaiming your power after narcissistic abuse is essential for your healing and growth. The manipulation and gaslighting tactics used by narcissists can leave you feeling powerless and stripped of your autonomy. By reclaiming your power, you take back control of your life and break free from the toxic grip of the abuser. It's about asserting your boundaries, standing up for yourself, and refusing to be a victim any longer. Reclaiming your power allows you to rebuild your self-esteem, regain your confidence, and rediscover your sense of worthiness. It's a vital step in your journey toward healing and creating a life that is authentically yours.

Murphy managed to reclaim his power after leaving Lisa. Let's drink from his cup of experience.

You know, when I first got out of that toxic relationship, I felt like I was drowning in a sea of lies. The narcissistic abuse had twisted my perception of reality, and I found myself believing all sorts of falsehoods about myself. It was like a constant loop of negative self-talk was playing in my head, telling me I wasn't good enough, didn't deserve love, and was to blame for everything that went wrong.

But one day, I decided enough was enough. I sat down and really listened to those lies, and I realized that they weren't truths at all. They were just echoes of the narcissist's manipulation, designed to keep me small and under their control. Once I identified those lies for what they were, I could start challenging them.

I started to question how those false beliefs were impacting my relationships. I saw how they were holding me back from forming meaningful connections with others and causing me to doubt the intentions of those who cared about me. It was like I was wearing a pair of tinted glasses that distorted everything I saw, and I knew I had to take them off if I wanted to see the world clearly again.

So, I made a conscious effort to replace those lies with truths. I reminded myself of my worth, my strengths, and all the things that made me unique. It wasn't easy, and there were days when I slipped back into old thinking patterns, but I kept pushing forward. Slowly but surely, I started to reclaim my power.

Learning new skills was a game-changer for me. It was like I was permitting myself to rewrite the script of my life, to challenge those false thoughts and behaviors that had kept me trapped for so long. Whether learning about mindfulness, practicing assertive communication, or honing my problem-solving skills, each new skill I acquired empowered me to take back control of my life.

Connecting with my community was another vital step in my healing journey. I found solace in sharing my story with others who had been through similar experiences. It was comforting to know that I wasn't alone and that there were people out there who understood what I was going through. Surrounding myself with supportive, empathetic individuals helped me feel seen, heard, and validated.

Taking care of my health became a top priority for me as well. I realized I needed to nourish my body, mind, and soul if I wanted to fully recover from the trauma of narcissistic abuse. I started prioritizing self-care activities like exercising regularly, eating nutritious foods, getting enough sleep, and practicing mindfulness and meditation. These simple yet powerful acts of self-love helped me rebuild my strength, resilience, and sense of well-being.

I learned to trust myself again, set boundaries, and stand up for what I deserved. I stopped letting those lies control me and instead took control of my own narrative. It was liberating, empowering, and incredibly freeing. And now, I want you to know you can do the same. You have the strength within you to reclaim your power and break free from the chains of narcissistic abuse. You just have to believe in yourself and take that first step forward.

CULTIVATE SELF-AWARENESS AFTER HEALING

Cultivating self-awareness after healing from narcissistic abuse is like shining a light into the darkest corners of your soul. It's about peeling back the layers, examining the wounds, and understanding the web of emotions and thoughts shaping your experiences.

Self-reflection is crucial during this journey because it helps you understand the dynamics of narcissistic abuse. By reflecting on past interactions and patterns, you can gain insights into how the abuse unfolded, how it affected you, and how you responded to it. This understanding is essential for breaking free from the grip of manipulation and reclaiming your power.

Validating your emotions is another important aspect of self-awareness. Many survivors of narcissistic abuse struggle with feelings of guilt, shame, and self-doubt. Self-reflection allows you to acknowledge and validate these emotions, recognizing they are a natural response to the trauma you've endured. Validating your emotions empowers you to release the burden of self-blame and embrace self-compassion instead.

Self-awareness also helps break the cycle of abuse. By examining your thoughts, beliefs, and behaviors, you can identify any lingering patterns of codependency or toxic dynamics in your relationships. This awareness enables you to set healthy boundaries, communicate effectively, and make empowered choices that prioritize your well-being.

Self-awareness allows you to rebuild your identity. Rebuilding self-identity is like piecing together a puzzle, one fragment at a time. It's about rediscovering who you are beyond the shadow of abuse and reconnecting with your passions, interests, and values. Through self-reflection and exploration, you can rebuild a strong and authentic sense of self that honors your true essence.

Additionally, self-awareness is a channel for self-care. Promoting self-care is an act of self-love and compassion. It involves prioritizing your physical, emotional, and mental well-being and nurturing yourself with kindness and tenderness. Self-care can take many forms, from practicing mindfulness and meditation to engaging in activities that bring you joy and relaxation. Making self-care a non-negotiable part of your daily routine empowers you to thrive and flourish.

As you cultivate self-awareness, pay attention to patterns and behaviors that signal potential toxicity in relationships. Trust your instincts and intuition, and don't ignore warning signs or dismiss your concerns. By recognizing red flags early on, you can prevent yourself from falling into familiar patterns of abuse and manipulation.

But how do I cultivate this self-awareness? Here is more of Murphy sharing his experience on how he managed to cultivate self-awareness:

Cultivating self-awareness was like navigating through a dense fog for me. At first, everything seemed murky and uncertain, but with time and patience, clarity began to emerge. I found that the journey of self-awareness starts with introspection, taking a closer look at your thoughts, feelings, and behaviors.

Journaling became a powerful tool for self-reflection for me. Every evening, I would sit down with my journal and pour out my thoughts onto the pages. I allowed myself to express whatever was on my mind without judgment or inhibition. Through writing, I uncovered hidden emotions, unearthed limiting beliefs, and gained insights into my inner world. Alongside journaling, mindfulness practices play a crucial role in cultivating self-awareness. I started incorporating mindfulness meditation into my daily routine, carving out moments of stillness and silence to simply be present with myself. These moments of mindfulness allowed me to observe my thoughts and emotions with greater clarity without getting swept away by them.

Another key aspect of fostering self-awareness was seeking feedback from trusted friends and mentors. I reached out to people whose perspectives I valued and asked for their honest reflections on my behavior and interactions. Their insights provided valuable mirrors, helping me gain a deeper understanding of myself and how I showed up in the world.

Through these practices and many others, I gradually cultivated a deeper sense of self-awareness. I learned to recognize my triggers, understand my patterns, and navigate my emotions with greater ease. Cultivating self-awareness wasn't always easy, but the journey was transformative, empowering me to live more authentically and intentionally.

EMBRACE YOUR FREEDOM

Embracing your freedom after escaping narcissistic abuse is not just about physical liberation; it's about reclaiming your autonomy, reclaiming your voice, and reclaiming your right to live life on your terms.

Many survivors of narcissistic abuse find themselves trapped in a psychological prison long after physically leaving their abuser. This phenomenon, known as Stockholm Syndrome, can make it challenging to break free from the mental shackles of the past.

However, embracing your freedom is crucial for several reasons. Firstly, it allows you to reconnect with your authentic self and rediscover the person you were before the abuse. By embracing your freedom, you reject the false narratives and manipulative tactics of your abuser, choosing instead to define yourself on your terms.

Embracing your freedom empowers you to set healthy boundaries and prioritize your well-being. It enables you to make choices that align with your values and desires rather than catering to the demands of others.

Additionally, embracing your freedom opens the door to new possibilities and opportunities for growth. It allows you to pursue your passions, explore your interests, and cultivate meaningful connections with others who support and uplift you.

Murphy narrates how he was able to embrace his newfound freedom:

> After escaping the toxic grip of narcissistic abuse, I realized that embracing my newfound freedom was essential for my healing journey.
> I started by envisioning the life I wanted—a life filled with joy, purpose, and fulfillment. I set clear goals and worked toward making my vision a reality. Along the way, I stopped seeking validation from others and started prioritizing my happiness and well-being. I realized that my worth wasn't dependent on the opinions of others.
> Taking a hard look at the beliefs and behaviors holding me back, I confronted and overcame these obstacles. Whether it was fear, self-doubt, or past trauma, I made a conscious effort to address them head-on. Through this process, I learned to embrace

my flaws and celebrate my strengths, treating myself with kindness and compassion.

Stepping out of my comfort zone became regular as I pursued my dreams and passions. I took risks, embraced the unknown, and trusted in my ability to handle whatever challenges came my way. Setting boundaries and saying no to anything that didn't align with my values became second nature. I prioritized my needs and desires without guilt or hesitation. Challenging the limiting beliefs ingrained in me during the abusive relationship was a crucial step. I replaced negative self-talk with positive affirmations and rewired my brain to believe in my worth and potential. Embracing a more carefree attitude, I let go of the need to control every aspect of my life and trusted in the process.

Through determination and perseverance, I discovered a renewed sense of purpose and joy in life. Embracing my newfound freedom allowed me to reclaim my power after narcissistic abuse, paving the way for a brighter and more fulfilling future.

PROCESSING NARCISSISTIC ABUSE

Recovery from narcissistic abuse is a journey that involves introspection, understanding, and healing. To aid you in this process, here are five reflective journal prompts designed to help you reflect on your experiences, emotions, and growth. Take your time with each prompt, allowing yourself to delve deep into your thoughts and feelings. By engaging with these prompts, you can gain valuable insights into your journey of healing and empowerment:

1. Reflect on the manipulation tactics used against you. How did they make you feel? Did you recognize them at the time, or did you only realize them in hindsight?
2. Think back to moments when you felt your boundaries were violated. How did you respond? What changes would you make now to better protect your boundaries in the future?
3. Consider the impact of the abuse on your self-esteem and self-worth. How has it influenced the way you perceive yourself? What steps can you take to rebuild your confidence?
4. Recall instances when you felt invalidated or gaslighted by the narcissist. How did you navigate these situations? How can you trust your intuition and instincts more moving forward?
5. Reflect on the aftermath of leaving the abusive relationship. What emotions have surfaced since then? How can you practice self-compassion and forgiveness as you continue to heal?

As we continue our journey of healing and self-discovery, Chapter 7 awaits with valuable insights and strategies to help us unravel and fix negative patterns that may have emerged from our experiences with narcissistic abuse. Get ready to dive deeper into your healing process and emerge stronger and more resilient than ever before.

U—UNRAVEL AND FIX NEGATIVE PATTERNS

"It takes but one positive thought, when given a chance to survive and thrive, to overpower an entire army of negative thoughts."

ROBERT H. SCHULLER

In Chapter 2, we probed into Christy's story—a narrative that resonates with many who have experienced narcissistic abuse. Christy, once confident and vibrant, found herself trapped in a web of manipulation and gaslighting, her sense of self eroded by her partner's relentless tactics. As she shared her struggles, a glimmer of hope emerged—a determination to break free from the shadow of her abuser and reclaim her power.

Christy continues to share with us her struggles with feelings of anxiety and negative thoughts.

Each morning, I woke up with a knot of anxiety in my stomach. It was like a dark cloud hovered over me, casting shadows on every aspect of my life. I doubted myself constantly, questioning every decision I made. "Am I good enough?" "Will they like me?" These thoughts plagued my mind, robbing me of peace and happiness.

Simple tasks became monumental challenges. Going to the grocery store felt like an insurmountable hurdle. I was terrified of running into someone I knew because I feared they could see right through me—see the broken person I had become. Social interactions were even worse. I found myself avoiding friends and family, convinced that they judged me as harshly as I judged myself.

The worst part was the negative beliefs about myself that seemed to be on an endless loop in my head. My partner's voice had become my inner voice: "You're worthless," "No one will ever love you," "You're a failure." These words were etched into my mind, replaying over and over until I started to believe them. But it wasn't just about me; my trust in others was shattered. I viewed every new person I met through a lens of suspicion and fear. I was convinced that everyone had ulterior motives, that everyone was out to hurt me. This paranoia isolated me further, making it even harder to break free from the cycle of anxiety and negative thinking.

One day, I hit rock bottom. I realized I couldn't live like this anymore. I needed to change, but I didn't know how. That's when I decided to seek help. I learned about cognitive behavioral therapy (CBT) and how it could help me challenge and change these destructive thought patterns.

Christy's journey is evidence of the profound impact of narcissistic abuse on mental health, but it also highlights a crucial turning point: the decision to seek help and commit to change. As we move forward, let's explore how overcoming the pattern of anxiety can pave the way for healing and reclaiming your life.

OVERCOME THE PATTERN OF ANXIETY

No one loves the idea of living on the edge, constantly battling a sense of dread with each passing day. Yet, for those who have experienced narcissistic abuse, this unsettling feeling can become a daily reality. It's as if your mind is perpetually stuck in survival mode, anticipating the next emotional ambush.

Anxiety is more than just feeling stressed or worried. It's an intense, persistent feeling of fear or apprehension about what's to come. Unlike regular worry that everyone experiences from time to time, anxiety can dominate your thoughts and impair your ability to function normally. It's like a mental fog that clouds your judgment and drains your energy.

Narcissistic abuse creates a fertile ground for anxiety to flourish. When you're in a relationship with a narcissist, you're subjected to constant manipulation, gaslighting, and emotional volatility. This unpredictable environment keeps you on high alert, never knowing when the next attack will come. Over time, your body and mind become conditioned to this state of hypervigilance, leading to chronic anxiety.

Recognizing the symptoms of anxiety is the first step toward overcoming it. Here are some common signs that anxiety may be affecting you:

- Feeling anxious about a wide range of issues, often without a clear cause
- Being unable to relax or sit still
- Feeling excessively tired despite getting enough sleep
- Finding it hard to focus on tasks or remember things
- Getting easily frustrated or angry
- Experiencing tightness or aches in your muscles
- Having trouble falling or staying asleep or experiencing restless sleep

Living in the shadow of anxiety is draining, but it's not a life sentence. You have the power to overcome it and reclaim your peace of mind. Christy, who struggled deeply with anxiety after her narcissistic relationship, managed to break free from its grip. Here's how she did it and how you can, too.

Recognize and Validate Your Feelings

Christy's first step was to acknowledge her anxiety. Instead of dismissing her feelings or blaming herself, she recognized that her anxiety was a natural response to the trauma she endured.

Christy says: "I used to berate myself for feeling anxious. But once I started acknowledging my feelings and accepting them without judgment, it was like a weight lifted off my shoulders. I realized that my anxiety wasn't my fault; it was a symptom of the abuse I had suffered."

Practice Mindfulness and Grounding Techniques

Mindfulness helped Christy stay present and reduce her anxiety. She practiced grounding techniques to calm herself during anxious moments.

Christy shares: "Whenever I felt anxiety creeping in, I focused on my breathing. I practiced grounding techniques, like naming five things I could see, four things I could touch, three things I could hear, two things I could smell, and one thing I could taste. It helped me stay present and break the cycle of anxious thoughts."

Establish a Routine

Creating a daily routine provided Christy with a sense of stability and control, which was crucial in managing her anxiety.

Christy explains: "Having a routine gave me something to rely on. It included regular sleep patterns, healthy meals, exercise, and time for relaxation. Knowing what to expect each day reduced my overall anxiety."

Challenge Negative Thoughts

Christy learned to identify and challenge the negative thoughts that fueled her anxiety.

Christy recounts: "I started keeping a journal where I would write down my anxious thoughts and then counter them with rational responses. It was a way of talking back to my anxiety and dismantling the lies it told me."

Engage in Physical Activity

Physical activity became a crucial part of Christy's anxiety management. Exercise helped her release built-up tension and improve her mood.

Christy says: "I started with simple activities like walking and gradually incorporated more vigorous exercises like yoga and cycling. The endorphin boost was a natural antidote to my anxiety."

Seek Professional Help

Christy sought the help of a therapist who specialized in trauma and anxiety. Professional guidance was instrumental in her healing journey.

Christy advises: "Talking to a therapist provided me with tools and strategies to manage my anxiety. It was empowering to have a professional validate my experiences and guide me through the healing process."

Connect with Supportive People

Building a support network of understanding and empathetic individuals helped Christy feel less isolated.

Christy reflects: "I surrounded myself with friends and family who understood my journey. Their support and encouragement were invaluable. I also joined a support group where I met others who had similar experiences, and we helped each other heal."

OVERCOME NEGATIVE THINKING PATTERNS AND LIMITING BELIEFS

Limiting beliefs are deeply ingrained convictions that constrain your potential. They are the mental barriers that tell you what you can't do, who you can't be, and what you don't deserve. These beliefs often form from past experiences and are perpetuated by negative thinking patterns.

Limiting beliefs can vary widely, but here are some common examples:

- "I'm not good enough."
- "I don't deserve to be happy."
- "I'll never succeed at this."
- "People will always let me down."
- "I'm unlovable."

These beliefs act as self-fulfilling prophecies, keeping you in a cycle of negativity and preventing you from pursuing opportunities for growth and happiness.

Narcissistic abuse dismantles your self-esteem and distorts your perception of reality. Narcissistic partners often criticize and belittle you to undermine your confidence and make you dependent on their approval. Over time, you start to internalize these negative messages and believe them to be true.

Narcissists frequently use gaslighting to make you question your reality, memory, and sanity. This manipulation can make you doubt your judgment and capabilities, reinforcing limiting beliefs.

As we already know, narcissists often control and isolate their victims, cutting off their support systems. Without external validation and perspective, it's easy to fall into a pattern of negative self-talk and limiting beliefs.

Narcissistic abuse often involves emotional manipulation, where your feelings are invalidated, and your worth is constantly questioned. This erosion of self-worth creates fertile ground for limiting beliefs to take root.

Let's turn to Christy, who faced the daunting task of overcoming deeply ingrained, limiting beliefs after escaping her narcissistic relationship. Through her journey, we can see how she dismantled these barriers and transformed her thinking patterns.

Recognizing Limiting Beliefs

Christy's first step was to identify her limiting beliefs. She realized that many of her thoughts about herself were not based on reality but were the echoes of her abuser's voice. Christy recalls:

> I started writing down the negative thoughts that would pop into my head. "I'm not good enough," "I can't do anything right," "No one will ever love me"— these were all things my ex had told me repeatedly. Seeing them on paper made me realize they weren't truths but the lies I'd been conditioned to believe.

Challenging and Reframing Beliefs

Once Christy identified her limiting beliefs, she began to challenge and reframe them. This involved questioning their validity and replacing them with positive affirmations. Christy shares:

> I asked myself, "Is this really true?" and "What evidence do I have to support this belief?" Most of the time, I found there was no real evidence, just the words of my abuser. I started replacing these thoughts with affirmations like, "I am capable," "I deserve love and respect," and "I am enough." It was a gradual process, but it significantly impacted how I viewed myself.

Surrounding Herself with Positivity

Christy also surrounded herself with positive influences. She sought out friends, family, and support groups that uplifted and encouraged her, helping to reinforce her new, positive beliefs. Christy reflects:

> I distanced myself from anyone who made me feel less than. Instead, I connected with people who believed in me and reminded me of my worth. Their support was invaluable in reshaping my self-image.

Practicing Self-Compassion

A crucial part of Christy's healing was learning to treat herself with kindness and compassion. She recognized that her journey was unique and that she needed to be patient with herself. Christy explains:

I used to be so critical of myself, but I realized I needed to become my own best friend. I started practicing self-compassion, forgiving myself for past mistakes, and celebrating my progress, no matter how small. This shift in mindset helped me break free from the grip of limiting beliefs.

Worksheet: Identifying Negative Thought Patterns

This worksheet is designed to help you identify and challenge negative thoughts so you can begin to replace them with healthier, more constructive ones. Completing this exercise can help you figure out where you might be making inaccurate assumptions or jumping to false conclusions.

Part 1: Identifying Negative Thoughts

Instructions: Take a moment to reflect on your recent thoughts, especially those that caused you stress or discomfort. Write down a few negative thoughts you've had in the past week.

1. ____

2. ____

3. ____

4. ____

5. ____

Part 2: Analyzing Negative Thoughts

Instructions: For each negative thought you've written down, answer the following questions to analyze and understand these thoughts better.

What triggered this thought?

Thought 1: _______________________________________

Thought 2: _______________________________________

Thought 3: _______________________________________

Thought 4: _______________________________________

Thought 5: _______________________________________

What emotions did this thought cause?

Thought 1: _______________________________________

Thought 2: _______________________________________

Thought 3: _______________________________________

Thought 4: _______________________________________

Thought 5: _______________________________________

What evidence supports this thought?

Thought 1: _______________________________________

Thought 2: _______________________________________

Thought 3: _______________________________________

Thought 4: _______________________________________

Thought 5: _______________________________________

What evidence contradicts this thought?

Thought 1: ____

Thought 2: ____

Thought 3: ____

Thought 4: ____

Thought 5: ____

Part 3: Challenging Negative Thoughts

Instructions: Use the answers from Part 2 to challenge and reframe each negative thought.

Is this thought based on facts or feelings?

Thought 1: ____

Thought 2: ____

Thought 3: ____

Thought 4: ____

Thought 5: ____

What would you say to a friend who had this thought?

Thought 1: ____

Thought 2: ____

Thought 3: ____

Thought 4: ____

Thought 5: ____

What is a more balanced or realistic way of thinking about this situation?

Thought 1: ____

Thought 2: ____

Thought 3: ____

Thought 4: ____

Thought 5: ____

Part 4: Creating Positive Alternatives

Here are ten affirmations to incorporate into your daily routine. Repeat these to yourself regularly, especially when you feel negative thoughts creeping in.

- I am worthy of love and respect.
- I am in control of my thoughts and emotions.
- I deserve happiness and fulfillment in my life.
- I am strong, resilient, and capable of overcoming challenges.
- My past does not define my future.
- I am growing and learning every day.
- I trust myself and my decisions.
- I am proud of who I am becoming.
- I attract positive and supportive people into my life.
- I am enough, just as I am.

Instructions: Transform each negative thought into a positive or neutral statement.

Positive Alternative:

Thought 1: _______________________________________

Thought 2: _______________________________________

Thought 3: _______________________________________

Thought 4: _______________________________________

Thought 5: _______________________________________

Conclusion: Identifying and challenging negative thought patterns is a powerful step toward improving your mental health and well-being. Regularly completing this exercise can help you develop a more positive and realistic outlook on life.

HOW CBT CAN HELP WITH HEALING

Christy mentioned she learned about CBT and how it could help her cope with her anxiety and overcome limiting beliefs:

When I first started CBT, I was filled with doubts. Could talking really make a difference? But as I worked with my therapist, I began to see how my thoughts were shaping my reality. I realized that believing I was "not good enough" was causing my anxiety and depression. My therapist taught me how to challenge these thoughts and replace them with positive affirmations like, "I am worthy of love and respect." Over time, these new thoughts began to feel more natural, and my confidence grew. I also learned to change my behavior by slowly facing social situations that I used to avoid. It wasn't an overnight change, but I started to reclaim my life step by step.

CBT is a type of talk therapy that focuses on identifying and changing negative thought patterns and behaviors. It's based on the concept that our thoughts, feelings, and behaviors are interconnected and that changing negative thoughts can lead to changes in feelings and behaviors.

CBT involves working with a therapist to recognize and challenge distorted thinking patterns and beliefs. Here's how it typically works:

- **Identify negative thoughts.** The first step is identifying the negative thoughts and beliefs causing distress. For Christy, this involved recognizing thoughts like "I am not good enough" or "I can't trust anyone."
- **Challenge negative thoughts.** Once identified, these thoughts are challenged. This means examining the evidence for and against them and considering alternative, more balanced thoughts. For example, Christy learned to challenge the thought "I am not good enough" by reminding herself of her accomplishments and strengths.
- **Replace negative thoughts.** The next step is to replace negative thoughts with positive or more realistic ones. Instead of thinking, "I am not good enough," Christy practiced thinking, "I am capable and deserving of love and respect."
- **Change your behavior.** CBT also involves changing behaviors that reinforce negative thoughts. For

example, if you avoid social situations because of anxiety, CBT would encourage gradual exposure to these situations in a safe and supportive way.

Understand that seeking therapy is not a sign of weakness but a brave step toward healing. Therapy provides a safe and supportive space to explore your thoughts and feelings, develop coping strategies, and rebuild your life. It's a valuable tool that can significantly aid your recovery journey.

In the next chapter, we will dive into how you can transcend the wounds inflicted by your past and build healthy, fulfilling relationships. Whether it's friendships, romantic relationships, or even familial ties, cultivating and maintaining positive connections is key to your continued healing and growth.

CHAPTER 8

T—TRANSCEND PAST WOUNDS AND BUILD HEALTHY RELATIONSHIPS

"Things end. People leave. And you know what? Life goes on. Besides, if bad things didn't happen, how would you be able to feel the good ones?"

ELIZABETH SCOTT

Recall Michaela from Chapter 4. Here is more of her story:

I couldn't shake the chill that gripped my heart. It had been two years since I had mustered the courage to leave my narcissistic ex-husband, yet the scars of our toxic relationship still lingered.

Every time I thought about opening my heart to someone new, fear clenched my chest like a vise. The memories of manipulation and abuse haunted me, leaving me paralyzed with doubt and suspicion. Could I ever trust again? Would I ever feel safe in another relationship?

As I scrolled through my phone, I couldn't help but notice the walls I had built around myself. I was cautious to a fault, scrutinizing every word and gesture for signs of deceit or manipulation. My friends had urged me to put myself out there, to give love another chance, but the thought filled me with dread.

In this chapter, we'll learn how to protect ourselves while remaining open to the possibility of genuine connection and love.

HOW TO RECOGNIZE AND AVOID RED FLAGS IN THE FUTURE

Here's a bitter fact: It's possible to escape from one narcissistic trap only to find yourself in another a couple of months later. I definitely don't wish this on you, but it's important to acknowledge the reality.

The ability to recognize and avoid red flags can be empowering and prevent you from falling into another narcissistic relationship. While it may be relatively easy to recognize these flags, it's a whole other challenge to avoid them. Many times, we see the warning signs but continue to compromise our boundaries, hoping things will improve or we will be able to change the other person. However, by actively avoiding these red flags and refusing to settle for less than we deserve, we reclaim our power and protect ourselves from further harm.

To fully understand how best we can recognize and avoid red flags in the future, let's listen to how Michaela has gone about her journey:

Trusting my intuition was the first step in reclaiming my power after leaving my narcissistic ex-husband. There were times when I met new people or found myself in unfamiliar situations, and something just didn't feel right. Instead of brushing off those feelings or convincing myself I was overreacting, I learned to lean into them.

For example, I remember meeting someone at a social gathering who seemed charming and charismatic at first glance. But as we talked, I noticed subtle inconsistencies in their stories and behavior. My gut told me something was off, so I decided to dig deeper instead of ignoring it.

I asked questions, observed their interactions with others, and paid attention to how they responded to boundaries. Sure enough, the more I probed, the more their true colors emerged. It became clear that this person was more interested in manipulation than genuine connection.

Looking for patterns was another crucial strategy I used to protect myself from falling into another narcissistic trap. After my experience with my ex-husband, I became hyper-aware of certain behaviors and attitudes that signaled potential danger.

For instance, whenever I encountered someone who seemed overly charming or excessively flattering, alarm bells would start ringing in my mind. I remembered how my ex-husband used flattery to disarm and manipulate me, so I became wary of anyone who employed similar tactics.

Similarly, I paid close attention to how people treated others, especially those in vulnerable positions.

Narcissists often show a lack of empathy and compassion, using and exploiting others for their own gain. Listening to the perspectives of my friends and family was a crucial aspect of my journey to avoid falling into another narcissistic relationship. After my experience with Joe, I realized that my judgment had been clouded by manipulation and gaslighting. I couldn't always trust my perceptions.

So, I consciously tried to lean on the people who cared about me and valued my well-being. Whenever I found myself drawn to someone new or uncertain about a particular situation, I sought the input of trusted friends and family members.

Their outside perspective often revealed things I hadn't noticed or acknowledged myself. They helped me see red flags that I might have overlooked or dismissed, providing invaluable insights into the true nature of certain individuals or dynamics.

Learning to listen to others wasn't always easy, especially when their observations contradicted my desires or hopes. But I recognized the importance of humility and open-mindedness in protecting myself from harm. Their input served as an additional defense against potential manipulation or abuse, and I'm grateful for their unwavering support throughout my journey.

Additionally, I dug into research and resources that shed light on the characteristics of narcissistic individuals. I learned about their tendencies toward grandiosity, entitlement, and a lack of accountability. Armed with this knowledge, I became more adept at identifying red flags and warning signs in potential partners or situations.

Recognizing these patterns became second nature to me. I could spot subtle cues and behaviors that hinted at narcissistic tendencies, allowing me to take proactive steps to protect myself. Rather than being blindsided by manipulation or gaslighting, I felt empowered by my newfound awareness and understanding.

To protect ourselves from narcissistic traps, we can watch out for numerous warning signs. To provide immediate insight, here is a Narcissist Red Flags Checklist. Keep it close, like a survival kit, ready to use when unsure about someone's intentions or behaviors. Here are some of the most common red flags:

- **Excessive Charm:** They come on strong with flattery and compliments, making you feel like the center of their universe too quickly.
- **Lack of Empathy:** They show little regard for your feelings, dismiss your emotions, or fail to understand your perspective.
- **Manipulation:** They use manipulation tactics such as gaslighting, guilt-tripping, or playing the victim to control and dominate you.
- **Entitlement:** They believe they are superior to others and deserve special treatment or attention.
- **Grandiosity:** They exaggerate their achievements, talents, or importance to gain admiration and validation.

- **Jealousy and Possessiveness:** They display extreme jealousy or possessiveness, trying to control who you spend time with or what you do.
- **Lack of Accountability:** They refuse to take responsibility for their actions, blaming others or external factors for their mistakes.
- **Boundary Violations:** They disregard your boundaries, invading your personal space or privacy without permission.
- **Mood Swings:** They exhibit unpredictable mood swings, alternating between extreme highs and lows.
- **Isolation:** They try to isolate you from your friends, family, or support network, making you dependent on them for validation and approval.

HOW TO TRUST AGAIN AND CONNECT INTIMATELY AND GENUINELY

You're absolutely right: Trusting again after experiencing the manipulative tactics of a narcissist can seem like an insurmountable challenge. But denying yourself the chance to love and trust again only gives your abuser continued power over you—something you've fought hard to break away from.

After enduring manipulation and betrayal in a narcissistic relationship, it's natural to develop trust issues. We may struggle to believe in the sincerity of others' intentions, leading to guardedness and skepticism in new relationships.

Narcissistic abusers often trample over boundaries, leaving us feeling violated and powerless. As a result, we may find it challenging to establish and enforce healthy boundaries in future relationships, fearing that asserting our needs will lead to conflict or rejection.

Narcissistic abuse can influence our attachment style, affecting how we relate to romantic partners. For example, those who experienced inconsistent or neglectful caregiving may develop anxious or avoidant attachment styles, impacting their ability to trust and connect in adult relationships.

While it's undoubtedly difficult, it is indeed possible to trust again and build genuine connections. It starts with understanding that the ability to love and trust is inherent in all of us, and it's a fundamental part of being human. So, how do you begin to trust again and connect intimately and genuinely?

Here are a couple of effective strategies and life hacks that Michaela found invaluable in rebuilding trust and fostering genuine connections at her own pace while prioritizing her well-being:

Creating distance was crucial for me in rebuilding trust and love again. After leaving my toxic relationship, I needed space to heal and rediscover myself. I focused on my well-being, engaging in activities that brought me joy and surrounding myself with supportive people. This distance allowed me to gain clarity and perspective, free from the influence of my past.

As I began to feel more grounded and confident, I cautiously opened up to new connections. I took things slowly, getting to know people at my own pace and allowing relationships to develop naturally. By prioritizing my needs and taking things one step at a time, I laid the foundation for trust and intimacy in my new relationships while protecting myself along the way.

Finding and cultivating relationships with individuals who offered safety was a game-changer for me. I sought out people who demonstrated empathy, respect, and understanding. These individuals created a supportive environment where I felt valued and heard.

By surrounding myself with such people, I gradually learned to trust again. Their consistent support and care helped me rebuild my confidence and belief in genuine connections. I allowed myself to be vulnerable, knowing they would honor and respect my boundaries.

Through these relationships, I discovered that trust can be earned over time through mutual respect and understanding. It wasn't about rushing into intimacy but building a foundation of trust and security. Finding and nurturing these relationships significantly impacted my journey toward healing and reconnecting with others.

Deliberately watching, tracking, and sometimes challenging the meanings I made of the kindness shown by these "safe" people was crucial in my journey. After experiencing narcissistic abuse, I developed the habit of second-guessing others' intentions and doubting genuine acts of kindness.

However, through mindfulness and self-awareness, I

learned to recognize and challenge these negative thought patterns. Instead of automatically assuming the worst, I started questioning whether my interpretations were based on past experiences or actual evidence.

For example, if someone offered me support or kindness, I would pause and reflect on their actions objectively. I asked myself whether there was any reason to doubt their sincerity or if my past trauma was influencing my perception.

BUILDING HEALTHY RELATIONSHIPS

Building healthy relationships is a significant milestone that signifies one's triumph over the pain and turmoil that once hindered personal growth. It represents a conscious effort to move beyond past traumas and cultivate connections based on trust, respect, and mutual support. By embarking on this journey, individuals demonstrate their resilience and commitment to their well-being.

Healthy relationships are characterized by open communication, empathy, and a genuine desire to understand and support each other. They provide a safe space where individuals can express themselves freely without fear of judgment or manipulation. Moreover, they foster emotional intimacy and connection, enriching the lives of all involved.

To build healthy relationships, stepping out of your comfort zone and being open to new experiences and connections is essential. However, the notion of "just putting yourself out there" can sometimes lead to repeating patterns of toxic relationships if healing hasn't taken place.

Rushing into new connections without addressing past wounds can leave you vulnerable to further pain and disappointment.

The key to building healthy relationships lies in prioritizing your healing journey. Healing takes time and patience, and it's crucial not to rush the process. Rushing through healing can result in bleeding onto the wrong people, overlooking those with genuine intentions, and repeating past mistakes.

Allowing yourself the necessary time and space to heal is vital for laying a solid foundation for healthy relationships. Healing involves introspection, self-reflection, and emotion. It's about understanding your triggers, recognizing harmful patterns, and learning to prioritize your well-being.

Identifying the type of relationship you want is crucial in building healthy connections. It involves clarifying your values, priorities, and what you're looking for in a relationship. This clarity helps you manage expectations and guides your actions and behaviors accordingly.

When you know what you want from a relationship, you're better equipped to communicate your needs and boundaries effectively. You can set clear expectations for yourself and others, which fosters honesty and transparency in your interactions.

Identifying the type of relationship you desire allows you to discern between healthy and unhealthy dynamics. You can recognize red flags more easily and make informed decisions about whom to invite into your life. This awareness empowers you to prioritize relationships that align with your values and contribute positively to your well-being.

By defining the kind of relationship you want, you're also setting intentions for the future. You're actively shaping the direction of your relationships and taking ownership of your romantic and interpersonal experiences. This proactive approach helps you attract partners and connections that resonate with your vision and goals.

Talking about your past relationship and speaking up if something reminds you of the abuse are essential aspects of building healthy connections. It's important to be open and honest about your experiences, even if they're difficult to discuss.

By sharing your past relationship experiences with a trusted partner, friend, or therapist, you're acknowledging your journey and seeking support in processing your emotions. This vulnerability allows you to release pent-up feelings and gain insights into your healing process.

Speaking up if something triggers memories of the abuse is crucial for your emotional well-being and boundary-setting. It's okay to assert yourself and communicate your discomfort or concerns when faced with reminders of past trauma. Your voice matters, and advocating for your needs reinforces your self-worth and agency. Discussing your past relationships and addressing triggers fosters understanding and empathy in your current connections. It helps your partner or loved ones comprehend your triggers and navigate sensitive topics with care and respect. This open communication strengthens trust and deepens your emotional bond.

While sharing your story, be mindful of your emotional state and boundaries. Take breaks if you feel overwhelmed, and prioritize self-care throughout the discussion. Healing is a personal journey, and it's okay to set limits on what you share and how much you disclose.

While at it, avoid comparing your current relationships to past ones. Each relationship is unique, and drawing parallels can hinder your ability to fully engage and connect with your present experiences. Instead, focus on understanding your past patterns and how they may influence your perceptions and behaviors moving forward.

Furthermore, when discussing your past experiences with others, be mindful of how you frame them. Choose language that empowers you and reflects your growth and resilience. Avoid victimizing yourself or assigning blame, as this can perpetuate feelings of powerlessness and inhibit your healing process.

EFFECTIVE COMMUNICATION AND SETTING BOUNDARIES

Effective communication and setting boundaries are foundational pillars of healthy relationships, yet they are often undermined in narcissistic dynamics. Narcissists typically struggle with effective communication skills and have little regard for personal boundaries, leading to a toxic cycle of manipulation and exploitation.

In your journey toward healing, you need to embody the opposite of narcissistic traits by prioritizing effective communication and establishing healthy boundaries.

Effective communication fosters understanding, empathy, and connection in relationships. By openly expressing your thoughts, feelings, and needs, you empower yourself to advocate for your well-being and cultivate authentic connections with others. In contrast, narcissists often employ tactics like gaslighting and manipulation to distort communication and maintain control over their victims.

Healthy boundaries are essential for maintaining autonomy, self-respect, and emotional safety. They define where you end and others begin, establishing clear parameters for acceptable behavior and interactions. Narcissists frequently disregard boundaries, crossing personal lines and infringing on others' autonomy for their benefit. By setting and enforcing boundaries, you assert your worth and protect yourself from exploitation and manipulation.

Assertive Communication

Assertive communication is characterized by the clear, direct, and respectful expression of one's thoughts, feelings, and needs while also acknowledging and respecting the rights and boundaries of others. It involves advocating for oneself confidently and constructively without resorting to aggression or passivity.

Let's consider two different individuals communicating with their partners:

Smith: "Um, hey, I was thinking maybe we could spend some time together this weekend. I mean, if that works for you. But, of course, if you have other plans or anything, it's totally fine."

Cole: "Hi, love. I'd like to talk about our plans for this weekend. I've been looking forward to spending some quality time together, and I was thinking it would be great to plan something special. I know we both have busy schedules, so I wanted to see if we could set aside some time to do something we both enjoy. What do you think?"

Do you notice the difference? Smith's communication lacks clarity and confidence. He hesitates and downplays his desire to spend time together, leaving the conversation open-ended and uncertain. It would sound like Smith has good intentions and wishes to spend time with his partner, yet at the same time, he gives alternatives and excuses.

To build and nourish lasting relationships, we ought to communicate like Cole. In Cole's message, he demonstrates several key aspects of effective communication:

- **Clarity:** Cole clearly expresses his intention to discuss plans for the weekend, leaving no room for ambiguity or misunderstanding.
- **Assertiveness:** By using phrases like "I'd like to talk" and "I was thinking," Cole asserts his desire to engage in a conversation about their plans. He expresses his own needs and preferences while acknowledging their busy schedules and showing consideration for himself and his partner.
- **Empathy:** Cole demonstrates empathy by acknowledging their busy schedules and suggesting they find a time that works for both of them. This shows that he values his partner's time and commitments.
- **Openness to collaboration:** Cole invites his partner's input by asking, "What do you think?" This encourages dialogue and collaboration, allowing both partners to contribute to the decision-making process.

Setting and Communicating Boundaries

Reflect on what is important to you and what you are comfortable with in your relationships. This could include boundaries around personal space, time commitments, communication preferences, and treatment by others.

When communicating your boundaries, be clear and specific about what you need or expect from others. Use assertive language and avoid being vague or ambiguous. For example:

- "I need some alone time in the evenings to recharge, so I'd appreciate it if we could limit our phone calls after 9 p.m."
- "It's important to me that we both contribute equally to household chores. Can we discuss a fair division of responsibilities?"

Frame your boundaries using "I" statements to take ownership of your feelings and needs without blaming others. This can help prevent defensiveness and promote understanding. For example:

- "I feel overwhelmed when I have too many commitments, so I need to prioritize my time more effectively."
- "I value honesty and transparency in our relationship, so I'd appreciate it if we could be open and honest with each other."

Clearly communicate the consequences of crossing your boundaries, but avoid making threats or ultimatums. Instead, focus on expressing how you will respond if your boundaries are not respected. For example:

- "If my need for space is consistently ignored, I may need to take some time apart to reevaluate our relationship."
- "If we're unable to find a compromise on this issue, I may need to seek support from a therapist to help us work through it."

Once you've communicated your boundaries, be sure to listen to and respect the boundaries of others. Healthy relationships require mutual respect and understanding of each other's needs and boundaries.

Starting small when setting boundaries is crucial because it allows you to gradually build confidence and assertiveness in your relationships. Going too big or making drastic changes all at once can be overwhelming and may even lead to resistance or backlash from others.

When you start with smaller boundaries, such as requesting alone time or expressing preferences in communication, you can gauge how others respond and adjust accordingly. This incremental approach gives you and the other person time to adapt and respect each other's needs without feeling pressured or threatened.

For example, instead of immediately setting a boundary around a major issue like finances or personal space, begin by addressing smaller concerns, such as asking for help with household chores or setting limits on phone calls or texts during certain times.

Starting small also allows you to practice assertive communication skills in less challenging situations, which can be applied to more significant boundary-setting conversations in the future. Over time, as you become more comfortable and confident in asserting your needs, you can gradually expand your boundaries to encompass larger aspects of your relationships.

SHARE YOUR STRENGTH

You're going to find a level of strength and resilience you didn't know you had in you as you move further through this journey. It may not feel like it now, but you will emerge stronger and more confident than you've ever been. Before you go, take a moment to help someone else get there too.

Simply by sharing your honest opinion of this book and, if you're comfortable, a little about your own experience, you'll help other people on their journey to heal from narcissistic abuse.

WANT TO HELP OTHERS?

Thank you so much for your support. There's a bright future ahead, and you're stronger than you realize.

Scan the QR code below.

CONCLUSION

Regarding the healing process, Michaela said:

> As I reflect on my journey, I realize that healing isn't a linear path; it's more like a cycle of growth and transformation. At each turn, I've shed layers of pain and emerged stronger, creating a better version of myself with each step. It's been about reclaiming my identity, rediscovering my worth, and embracing the freedom I've always yearned for.

Michaela's journey encapsulates the essence of the healing process, showcasing the cyclical nature of growth and renewal. Each phase, from acknowledging the aftermath to transcending past wounds, has been pivotal in her evolution. This journey speaks to the resilience of the human spirit and the power of self-discovery.

This book has been a journey of healing and empowerment, guiding you through the aftermath of narcissistic abuse toward a brighter future. The key takeaway is that healing is possible, and you hold the power to break free from toxic cycles. By embracing the BREAKOUT framework, you've gained the tools to reclaim your identity, rebuild your self-esteem, and cultivate healthy relationships.

BREAKOUT has been our roadmap to freedom and healing:

- **Break the façade.** We've uncovered the manipulative façade of the narcissist, freeing ourselves from their deceptive grasp.
- **Release yourself from manipulation and codependency.** By breaking the chains of manipulation and codependency, we've reclaimed our independence and autonomy.
- **Escape the narcissist's traps safely.** By safely navigating away from the traps set by the narcissist, we've shielded ourselves from further harm.
- **Acknowledge the aftermath.** By facing the aftermath of abuse head-on, we've accepted our pain and trauma, laying the foundation for healing.
- **Keep yourself holistically healthy.** By prioritizing our mental health, we've nurtured our well-being as we journey toward recovery.
- **Own your narrative.** By taking control of our stories, we've reclaimed our sense of self and identity.
- **Unravel and fix negative patterns.** By unraveling detrimental patterns and beliefs, we've replaced them with healthier, empowering ones.
- **Transcend past wounds and build healthy relationships.** Rising above past wounds, we've

forged relationships built on trust, respect, and mutual support.

This program has equipped us with the tools and resilience needed to transcend the pain of narcissistic abuse and build a brighter, healthier future.

It's not your fault that you experienced narcissistic abuse. The lies and manipulation you endured were not of your making. But now, armed with the insights and strategies from this book, you have the power to uncover those lies and reclaim your truth.

Healing from the trauma of narcissistic abuse is undoubtedly a challenging journey. But I want you to know, with every fiber of your being, that you are capable of it. You are worthy of healing, of happiness, and of a life free from the shackles of abuse.

With the knowledge and tools provided in these pages, you are equipped to recognize the signs of narcissistic abuse, to leave toxic relationships behind, to heal from the wounds inflicted upon you, and to move forward with strength and resilience.

You are not alone on this journey. Remember, you are worth every step of the healing process. Believe in yourself, trust in your resilience, and know that you deserve all the love and joy the world has to offer.

May this book serve as a guiding light on your path to healing and empowerment. You've got this.

Before we part ways, I want to ask a small favor. If you found this book helpful on your journey to healing from narcissistic abuse, would you leave a review on Amazon? Your feedback will help others find the support they need and mean the world to me.

Lastly, I want to extend my heartfelt wishes to you on your journey ahead. Healing from narcissistic abuse is no easy feat, but I believe in your strength and resilience. May you find the peace, healing, and happiness you deserve as you continue on your path.

With warmest regards,

Jackson Porter

REFERENCE

Arabi, Shahida. "11 Signs Youre the Victim of Narcissistic Abuse." Psych Central, August 21, 2017. https://psychcentral.com/blog/recovering-narcissist/2017/08/11-signs-youre-the-victim-of-narcissistic-abuse

Blinkist Magazine. "Quotes About Life Going On: Top 10 Inspirational Quotes to Keep Moving Forward," October 25, 2023. https://www.blinkist.com/magazine/posts/quotes-life-going-top-10-inspirational-quotes-keep-moving-forward

Bottaro, Angelica. "How to Recover From Narcissistic Abuse." Verywell Health, July 31, 2024. https://www.verywellhealth.com/narcissistic-abuse-recovery-challenges-and-treatment-5210945

Bouche, Hailey. "How to Spot the Bright Red Flags of a Narcissist." The Everygirl, November 22, 2023. https://theeverygirl.com/narcissist-red-flags/

Davis, Shirley. "Codependency and Narcissistic Abuse." *CPTSD Foundation* (blog), January 6, 2022. https://cptsdfoundation.org/2022/01/06/codependency-and-narcissistic-abuse/

Gupta, Sanjana. "How to Avoid Falling Into a Narcissistic Relationship Pattern." Verywell Mind, December 31, 2023. https://www.verywellmind.com/how-to-avoid-falling-into-a-narcissistic-relationship-pattern-5218950

"How to Recognize and Cope With Narcissist Discard." Verywell Mind, May 14, 2024. https://www.verywellmind.com/narcissistic-discard-causes-impact-and-coping-strategies-5218979

Herbal Goodness. "How to Make Effective and Potent Herbal Tinctures: A Comprehensive Guide," June 1, 2024. https://www.herbalgoodnessco.com/blogs/healthy-living

Holly, Kellie Jo. "Boundaries Are Crucial for Abuse Victims." Verbal Abuse Journals, May 23, 2012. https://verbalabusejournals.com/how-stop-abuse/boundaries-imperative-for-abuse-victims/

Jordan, Krista. "Breaking Up With a Narcissist: 5 Tips & What to Expect." Choosing Therapy, September 5, 2023. https://www.choosingtherapy.com/breaking-up-with-a-narcissist/

Joshi, Shivank. "150+ Toxic Family Quotes On Letting Go And Moving On."

MomJunction, December 22, 2021. https://www.momjunction.com/arti cles/toxic-family-quotes-and-sayings_00793638/

Keohan, Elizabeth. "Narcissistic Abuse: Examples, Signs, and Effects." *Talkspace* (blog), September 29, 2022. https://www.talkspace.com/mental-health/conditions/articles/narcissistic-abuse/

Leanjumpstart. "39 Positive Attitude Quotes to Stop Negative Thoughts + Free Cards," n.d. https://leanjumpstart.com/picture-quotes/positive-atti tude-quotes/

Loggins, Brittany. "Healing After Narcissistic Abuse: What Does Healing Look Like?" Verywell Mind, December 26, 2023. https://www.verywell mind.com/stages-of-healing-after-narcissistic-abuse-5207997

Lundberg, Amanda. "The Long-Term Effects of Narcissistic Abuse." Charlie Health, February 19, 2023. https://www.charliehealth.com/post/the-long-term-effects-of-narcissistic-abuse

Marriage Recovery Center. "Why Do Narcissists Act The Way They Do?," November 26, 2023. https://marriagerecoverycenter.com/why-do-narcissists-act-the-way-they-do/

Matt D, Fox. "Boundaries: 8 Rock Solid Ways to Set Them after Narcissistic Abuse." *Matt D Fox* (blog), n.d. https://www.mattdfox.com/boundaries-8-rock-solid-ways-to-set-them-after-narcissistic-abuse/

McGee, Jim. "How to Reclaim Your Identity After Narcissistic Abuse." *Jim McGee Coaching* (blog), April 12, 2023. https://jimmcgeecoaching.com/identity-after-narcissistic-abuse/

McNelis, Kelly. "14 Quotes That Will Inspire You to Share Your Story." Kelly McNelis, LLC, May 12, 2017. https://kellymcnelis.com/share-your-story-quotes/

Moore, Marissa. "Narcissist and Codependent Compatibility in Relationships." Psych Central, November 11, 2021. https://psychcentral.com/disorders/the-dance-between-codependents-narcissists

Muenter, Olivia. "145 Quotes About Narcissism to Know and Recognize." Woman's Day, June 14, 2022. https://www.womansday.com/life/a40059190/narcissist-quotes/

Neuharth, Dan. "25 Spot-On Quotations About Narcissism." Psych Central, August 15, 2017. https://psychcentral.com/blog/narcissism-decoded/2017/08/25-spot-on-quotations-about-narcissism

Odell, Cherrial Ann. "How Is Life Tree(Ting) You?: Trust, Safety, and Respect - The Importance of Boundaries | Student Affairs." Stanford Student Affairs, n.d. https://studentaffairs.stanford.edu/how-life-treet ing-you-importance-of-boundaries

Pace, Rachael. "How to Have a Healthy Relationship After Emotional Abuse." Marriage.com, December 4, 2023. https://www.marriage.com/advice/relationship/how-to-have-a-healthy-relationship-after-emotional-abuse/

Quinlan, Calantha. "Forgiving Yourself After Narcissistic Abuse: 10 Kind Tips." Marriage.com, April 2, 2024. https://www.marriage.com/advice/mental-health/forgiving-yourself-after-narcissistic-abuse/

Raypole, Crystal. "Are You Codependent? Here Are the Key Signs of Codependency." Psych Central, May 17, 2016. https://psychcentral.com/lib/symptoms-signs-of-codependency

Rice, Meaghan. "What to Know About Dating After Narcissistic Abuse." *Talkspace* (blog), December 28, 2023. https://www.talkspace.com/mental-health/conditions/articles/dating-after-narcissistic-abuse/

Saeed, Kim. "Give Your New Relationship a Fighting Chance After Narcissistic Abuse." Kim Saeed, July 27, 2023. https://kimsaeed.com/2023/07/27/give-your-new-relationship-a-fighting-chance-after-narcissistic-abuse/

"Healing from Identity Loss After Narcissistic Abuse." Psych Central, August 22, 2018. https://psychcentral.com/blog/liberation/2018/08/healing-from-identity-loss-after-narcissistic-abuse

Salmansohn, Karen. "11 Healing Narcissist Quotes If You're Hurt By Narcissistic Behavior." *NotSalmon* (blog), March 29, 2018. https://www.notsalmon.com/2018/03/29/quotes-about-narcissists/

Sarkis, Stephanie. "How To Regain Your Sanity After You've Been Gaslighted." mindbodygreen, March 12, 2021. https://www.mindbodygreen.com/articles/what-to-do-when-youve-been-gaslighted

Shaw, Elizabeth. "Removing Limiting Beliefs After Narcissistic Abuse." Overcoming Narcissistic Abuse, March 7, 2020. https://wasitme.blog/2020/03/07/removing-limiting-beliefs-after-narcissistic-abuse/

Sissons, Beth. "Narcissistic Abuse: Definition, Signs, and Recovery." Medical News Today, October 5, 2022. https://www.medicalnewstoday.com/articles/narcissistic-abuse

The Collaborative Counseling Center. "How To Heal From Gaslighting: A Therapist Explains Steps To Start Your Healing Process," September 30, 2021. https://www.collabcounseling.com/blog/how-to-heal-from-gaslighting-a-therapist-explains-steps-to-start-your-healing-process

Wakefield, Manya. "The Cycle of Narcissistic Abuse." Narcissistic Abuse Rehab, July 15, 2023. https://www.narcissisticabuserehab.com/cycle-of-narcissistic-abuse/